I0827976

IMAGES
of America

EMPORIUM DEPARTMENT STORE

On the Cover: Workmen install a new "Big E" sign at the Emporium on Market Street in 1964. (Photograph by Skelton Photography; courtesy of the San Francisco History Center, San Francisco Public Library.)

IMAGES
of America

EMPORIUM DEPARTMENT STORE

Anne Evers Hitz

ISBN 978-1-5316-7706-0

Published by Arcadia Publishing
Charleston, South Carolina

Library of Congress Control Number: 2014939713

For all general information, please contact Arcadia Publishing:
Telephone 843-853-2070
Fax 843-853-0044
E-mail sales@arcadiapublishing.com
For customer service and orders:
Toll-Free 1-888-313-2665

Visit us on the Internet at www.arcadiapublishing.com

To my family, especially my husband, Breck Hitz, my chief cheerleader; thanks for listening to all my stories about adventures in photograph research and San Francisco history.

Contents

Acknowledgments

So many people have fond memories of the Emporium and were supportive of this project. The Dohrmann-Evers-Pischel extended family—the descendents of F.W. Dohrmann—were especially enthusiastic about getting the story told. In particular, I would like to thank William D. Evers, Edwina Leggett, Elliot Evers, John Evers, William Dohrmann Evers Jr., Madeline Kerr, Karl and Karen Heisler, Al Evers, Stephanie Barbour, Kate Harrington, Dore Griffinger, Nancy Evers Kirwan, Barbara Barbour, Ava Jean Brumbaum, Bill Evers, Cathy Evers, Mark Dohrmann, and Geoff Dohrmann.

Other individuals who were very generous and contributed their memorabilia to the book include Ron Ross, Dorothy Rice, Pam Gibson, Harold Rudolph, Jim Dickson, Craig Sundstrom, Kathleen Manning, Scott Nimmo, Tony Ford, Louis Capecci, Heather David, John Plummer, Bruce Kopytek of the Department Store Museum website, Judy Skelton, and Alan Thomas.

The patient librarians who answered my endless questions deserve a thanks as well: Andrea Grimes, San Francisco History Center, San Francisco Public Library; Charlene Duval and Leilani Marshall, Sourisseau Academy for State and Local History; Kathleen Correia, California State Library; Nathan Kerr, Oakland Museum; Susan Snyder, Bancroft Library; the staff at the North Baker Research Library, California Historical Society; and Julie LaBenz and Ali Noyer of the Westfield Centre San Francisco.

Three books contributed greatly to my research, including two by Jan Whitaker, *Service and Style: How the American Department Store Fashioned the Middle Class* and *The World of Department Stores*. Richard Longstreth's *The American Department Store Transformed 1920–1960* also gave a great overview of why downtown department stores struggled as the suburbs grew.

I would also like to gratefully acknowledge the permission granted to reproduce the copyrighted material in this book. Every effort has been made to trace copyright holders and to obtain their permission for the use of copyrighted material. I apologize for any errors or omissions and would be grateful if notified of any corrections that should be incorporated in future reprints or editions of this book.

INTRODUCTION

At the end of the 19th century, grand emporiums dominated the retail landscape in cities across the United States. It was an era when the big stores and great merchants marched forward, becoming national institutions. On the East Coast, New York had, among many, Gimbel's, Abraham & Straus, A.T. Stewart's, and B. Altman & Company. Philadelphia had Strawbridge & Clothier and Wanamaker's. Chicago had its beloved Marshall Field's, Minneapolis its Dayton's, and, in Boston, Filene's was an institution.

Economic growth steadily expanded through the 19th century. People were moving to the cities, and the affluent middle class had money to spend, demanding more goods than the simple country store could provide. By end of the 19th century, there were almost 1,000 American department stores, many housed in beautiful buildings, with hundreds of thousands of shoppers a day coming through their doors. Window shopping became a leisure activity.

Almost anything could be bought in these department stores. What made a great department store? A central location serviced by mass transportation, a great variety of goods, lower prices, free services such as deliveries, liberal credit arrangements, and merchandise return privileges. The stores were strictly departmentalized, appealed to the masses, offered many services, and were big advertisers.

On the West Coast, the last half of the 19th century saw explosive growth in the population of San Francisco. As the world rushed to California in search of gold and fortune, the city's population increased exponentially, from less than 400 in 1847 to almost 30,000 by the end of 1849. By 1860, there were over 56,000 people, and, by 1890, the population approached 300,000, making San Francisco the eighth-largest city in the country. In the 1900 census, San Francisco was listed as the second-largest city west of the Mississippi, and the largest west of the Rockies.

With many new fortunes made, and the Barbary Coast in full swing, the Gold Rush introduced an air of prosperity, making San Francisco a cosmopolitan metropolis with a frontier edge. Access to San Francisco became easier when Oakland, across the bay, became the terminus of the Transcontinental Railroad, linking the east to the west, in 1869. Ferry service brought passengers over to San Francisco.

Entrepreneurs catering to the needs and tastes of the growing San Francisco population included Levi Strauss, who opened a dry goods business, and Domingo Ghirardelli, who manufactured his signature chocolate. Other early winners were the banking industry, with the founding of Wells Fargo in 1852 and the Bank of California in 1864. The burgeoning population needed schools, churches, theaters, and all goods for establishing households.

I. Magnin, City of Paris, the White House, the Emporium—these were the stores, all founded in the second half of the 19th century, where San Franciscans shopped. Only the Emporium, however, was located "south of the slot," on the south side of Market Street. The others clustered around Union Square, considered the classier area of town, although just a few blocks from Market Street and the Emporium.

There are many stories surrounding these San Francisco stores and the merchants who founded them in the years after the Gold Rush. The stores lining Union Square catered to the higher classes, and their owners looked to Paris for inspiration for their style and merchandising. City of Paris's founder, Felix Verdier, had arrived in May 1850 in the San Francisco harbor on a chartered ship, the *Ville de Paris* ("City of Paris"), loaded with silks, laces, fine wines, champagne, and cognac. San Francisco citizens, desperate for consumer goods, quickly surrounded the ship with rowboats and purchased all the goods before they could be unloaded from the ship, often paying with bags of gold dust. Dutch-born Mary Ann Magnin and her English husband, Isaac Magnin, founded I. Magnin. Mary Ann opened a shop in 1876 selling lotions and high-end clothing for infants. Later, she expanded into bridal wear. As her business grew, her exclusive clientele relied on her for the newest fashions from Paris. The White House store also had a Parisian emphasis (Raphael Weill, who owned it, was a French émigré). The White House maintained a buying office in Paris, and most of those in key management positions were from France, which meant that the store brought French style to San Francisco. For years, the store was also noted for its elegant tearoom.

The Emporium, on the other hand, aimed for a more middle-class clientele, and for many years since its founding in 1896 (and subsequent reorganization in 1897), it not only succeeded, it thrived, despite near-total destruction in the 1906 earthquake. After some business mishaps in the beginning, once the store was reorganized and managed as a single enterprise instead of a collection of individually owned small shops, it built a loyal clientele and was the place to go to shop, hear concerts, have a cup of tea, or visit Santa.

Despite many years of success, none of these San Francisco institutions survived, in spite of efforts to establish branch stores in the fast-growing suburbs. All were eventually absorbed by other companies or closed. The retail landscape had changed, customers shopped at chain discount stores, and the inner city declined. Women joined the workforce and no longer had the time or the inclination for a day-long shopping trip or to enjoy afternoon tea and a concert in a store.

Many native San Franciscans have fond memories of the "Big E." It was the place where they got their first grown-up jacket, shopped for back-to-school clothes, and rode the big slide or the train on the roof at Christmas, a time that also always meant a visit with Santa and a photograph. A trip downtown was something special that one dressed up for, and, in the 1950s, that meant gloves and a hat. While the department stores thrived, they also satisfied some basic needs beyond just retail consumption. Times change, however, and despite San Francisco's current economic upswing and the revitalization of Market Street, the grand downtown department stores no longer have a place in the retail panorama.

One

1896–1906
Getting Started

The Emporium's beginnings were rocky. In 1893, a German immigrant, Adolph Feist, leased the Parrott Building on Market Street with the idea of turning it into a large department store, hoping to interest an East Coast partner. Designed by San Francisco architect Albert Pissis, one of the first Americans to be trained at the École des Beaux Arts in Paris, the seven-story Parrott Building emulated the immense arcades of London and Paris. The concept of a "department store" was a new one, and Feist's original idea was to lease space to a variety of individual merchants without any centralized management.

In 1896, with great pomp, the Emporium opened. Some of the first businesses there were Nathan-Dohrmann & Co., selling china, glassware, lamps, and art goods; Kelly & Leibes, women's clothing; and Sing Fat & Co., a Chinese and Japanese bazaar. Offices, including those of the Supreme Court of California, occupied the upper floors.

Unfortunately, the original Emporium soon went bankrupt, primarily from its lack of centralized management. F.W. Dohrmann, another German immigrant and a partner at Nathan-Dohrmann & Co., saw possibilities in the project in spite of the general opinion that any department store on the south side of Market Street must fail. All the higher-end stores were on the north, near Union Square.

Despite the perception that stores on the south side of Market could not be successful, down the street, the Davis brothers successfully operated the Golden Rule Bazaar, which sold "toys, wheel goods, bicycles built for two, cutlery, dry goods and whatnots."

Dohrmann, along with his partners, secured the bankrupt Emporium and merged it with the Golden Rule Bazaar in the Parrott Building. The Emporium and Golden Rule Bazaar launched in September 1897.

F.W. Dohrmann and his son A.B.C. Dohrmann built the management systems and procedures for different departments to work together. Soon, a well-knit organization was thriving, and the store became a popular social as well as shopping center, with band concerts every Saturday night. From 1898 to 1906, an unbroken line of success moved the Emporium up among the leaders of the city's retail trade. In 1901, the Golden Rule Bazaar name was removed.

Market Street, seen here in 1899, San Francisco's main thoroughfare and the home of the Emporium, was the widest street in town at the time, at 120 feet. Three miles long, it cut across the city from the waterfront up to the hills of Twin Peaks. The grand boulevard connected the Ferry Building to growing neighborhoods via horse-drawn streetcar, and later via four clattering cable cars. (Photograph by B.L. Singley, Keystone View Co.; courtesy of the Library of Congress.)

This is a view looking down Powell Street toward Market and the Emporium in 1904. The owners of the Emporium had been warned that they would have little chance of success on the south side of Market, as the large stores were all on the north side. The success of the Emporium proved them wrong. (Courtesy of the San Francisco History Center, San Francisco Public Library.)

A parade passes by the Emporium (right). The card says it is a Labor Day parade, and it is copyright 1906, but the scene must be from the previous Labor Day in 1905, since Market Street was in post-earthquake shambles in 1906. (Courtesy of the Library of Congress.)

The Ringling Bros. Circus parades down Market Street in September 1900. As it grew in popularity, Market Street, with its wide boulevard cutting through the heart of the city, became the center of public celebrations. Formerly, parades and similar events were confined to Montgomery and Kearny Streets, or fashionable Stockton Street. But by the turn of the 20th century, all was changed, and scenes of this kind shifted to the big thoroughfare. (Courtesy of Wikimedia Commons.)

Union Square, seen here before the 1906 earthquake, was made into a public park in 1850. In the 1880s, the square became the center of a fashionable residential district. By the turn of the 20th century, offices and stores dominated the square, pushing out residences and churches. Located two blocks north of Market Street and the Emporium, it was, and still is, the center of San Francisco's retail district. (Photograph by Albert Dressler; courtesy of the California History Room, California State Library, Sacramento, California.)

The Emporium was an incredibly elegant store. The *San Francisco Chronicle* published an article on May 23, 1896, entitled "The Finest Store in All the World," which stated, "San Francisco's Palatial Structure Excels the Famous Bon Marchés of Paris . . . The first view of the Emporium and the interior . . . is dreamlike. There is a vast blaze of electricity . . . 10,000 lights—a vast expanse of white enameled wood that looks like marble, a street paved with a marble mosaic, as Pompeii was . . . everything is a creamy white, but the 4,000 electric lights fringe the dome with sparkling color." (Courtesy of the Bancroft Library, University of California, Berkeley, 91/29c ctn. 1:55.)

Albert Pissis (1852–1914), the Emporium's architect, introduced the Beaux Arts architectural style to San Francisco, designing a number of important buildings in the city in the years before and after the 1906 earthquake. In addition to the Emporium, Pissis designed the Hibernia Bank Building, the James Flood Building, the White House Department Store, and the Mechanics' Institute Library. The Emporium helped turn Market Street, with its excellent transportation, into a major shopping destination. These two photographs illustrate its pre-earthquake grandeur. (Above, courtesy of Louis Capecci; below, courtesy of the Westfield San Francisco Centre.)

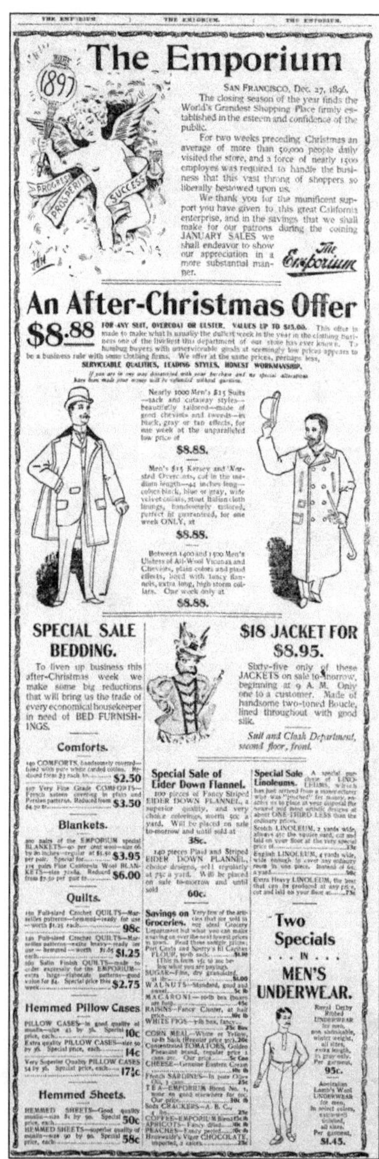

The Emporium

1897

San Francisco, Dec. 27, 1896.

The closing season of the year finds the World's Grandest Shopping Place firmly established in the esteem and confidence of the public.

For two weeks preceding Christmas an average of more than 50,000 people daily visited the store, and a force of nearly 1500 employes was required to handle the business that this vast throng of shoppers so liberally bestowed upon us.

We thank you for the munificent support you have given to this great California enterprise, and in the savings that we shall make for our patrons during the coming JANUARY SALES we shall endeavor to show our appreciation in a more substantial manner.

The Emporium

PROGRESS PROSPERITY SUCCESS

An After-Christmas Offer

$8.88

SERVICEABLE QUALITIES, LEADING STYLES, HONEST WORKMANSHIP.

Nearly 1000 Men's $15 Suits—sack and cutaway styles—beautifully tailored—made of good cheviots and tweeds—in black, gray or fan effects, for one week at the unparalleled low price of

$8.88.

Men's $15 Kersey and Worsted Overcoats, cut in the medium length—42 inches long—colors black, blue or gray, wide velvet collars, stout Italian cloth linings, handsomely tailored, perfect fit guaranteed, for one week ONLY, at

$8.88.

Between 1400 and 1500 Men's Ulsters of All-Wool Vicunas and Cheviots, plain colors and plaid effects, lined with fancy flannels, extra long, high storm collars. One week only at

$8.88.

SPECIAL SALE BEDDING.

To liven up business this after-Christmas week we make some big reductions that will bring us the trade of every economical housekeeper in need of BED FURNISHINGS.

Comforts.

$2.50

$3.50

Blankets.

$3.95

$6.00

Quilts.

98c

$1.25

$2.75

Hemmed Pillow Cases

10c

14c

17½c

Hemmed Sheets.

50c

58c

$18 JACKET FOR $8.95.

Sixty-five only of these JACKETS on sale to-morrow, beginning at 9 A. M. Only one to a customer. Made of handsome two-toned Boucle, lined throughout with good silk.

Suit and Cloak Department, second floor, front.

Special Sale of Eider Down Flannel.

38c.

60c.

Special Sale Linoleums.

Savings on Groceries.

Two Specials ... IN ... MEN'S UNDERWEAR.

95c.

$1.45.

This ad from June 1897 appeared before the merger with the Golden Rule Bazaar. In the banner, through the logo, it reads, "Sixty Stores Under One Roof." By later in that year, after bankruptcy, the Emporium had merged with the Bazaar and had streamlined its management and departments, no longer focusing on different stores. (Courtesy of the Library of Congress, Chronicling America.)

In this post-Christmas advertisement, the store—"The World's Grandest Shopping Place"—thanks its customers for their 1896 holiday patronage, saying that an average of 50,000 people visited the store daily, and 1,500 employees worked to handle the "vast throng of shoppers so liberally bestowed upon us." (Courtesy of the Library of Congress, Chronicling America.)

THE SAN FRANCISCO CALL, TUESDAY, JUNE 1, 1897.

The Emporium

MARKET STREET SAN FRANCISCO CAL

CLOSING OUT SALE IN ALL DEPARTMENTS.

ALL PRICES ON SALE GOODS WILL BE MARKED IN RED INK.

Fine Dresses, Jackets.

Millinery.

Dress Goods

Children's and Infants' Clothing

Wash and Silk Waists.

Ladies' Underwear.

Fine Furniture.

Blankets.

Black Dress Goods.

Handkerchiefs, Ladies' Neckwear.

Emb'deries.

Men's and Ladies' Shoes.

Comforts.

House Furnishings

Carpets and Rugs.

CROCKERY, GLASSWARE, LAMPS.

Finest Oriental Bazaar in America.

In these pre-earthquake images, one can see why the Emporium was the place to go, not only for shopping, but also for concerts "under the Dome." The store had its own orchestra, with John Marquardt as director and Mrs. Marquardt as harpist. Concerts were held three times a week on the elevated bronze stand. (Above, courtesy of Ron Ross; below, photograph by Louis J. Stellman, courtesy of the California History Room, California State Library, Sacramento, California.)

These images gives a sense of the grandeur of the Emporium's center court, the glorious dome perched atop the building, the interior with its balconies and departments, and the stand in the middle with its café and bandstand. Marble, bronze, steel, and polished mahogany were used throughout the store. The ground floor was over 96,000 square feet, and the rotunda was 140 feet in diameter. A total of 125 tons of steel were used in the dome, 15 elevators serviced the upper floors, and over 50 miles of electric wire were installed. (Above, courtesy of Pam Gibson; below, courtesy of the California Historical Society, CHS2013.1455.)

Frederick W. "F.W." Dohrmann (1842–1914), "the Busiest Man in San Francisco," was a German immigrant who settled in San Francisco in 1862. Instrumental in helping reorganize the Emporium into a prosperous department store with centralized management, he said, "To make such an enterprise profitable . . . it is necessary that we should have INTELLIGENT LEADERSHIP, PERFECT ORGANIZATION and AMPLE CAPITAL . . . we must: ORGANIZE, CAPITALIZE, HARMONIZE, SYSTEMATIZE, ECONOMIZE and ADVERTISE." Dohrmann was involved in many commercial and civic ventures, including helping organize the San Francisco Hotel Company, which operated the St. Francis Hotel, and leading the Merchants' Association. He served as a director for several of the Dohrmann Commercial Company's stores, as a member of the Park Commission, and as a University of California regent. (Right, courtesy of the Bancroft Library, University of California, Berkeley, 1991.076—PIC Folder 1; below, courtesy of *San Francisco Chronicle*, October 4, 1903.)

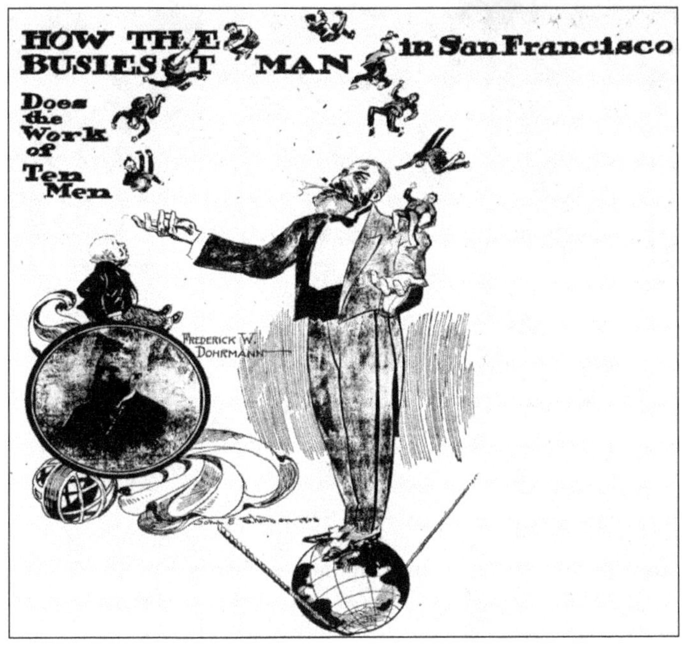

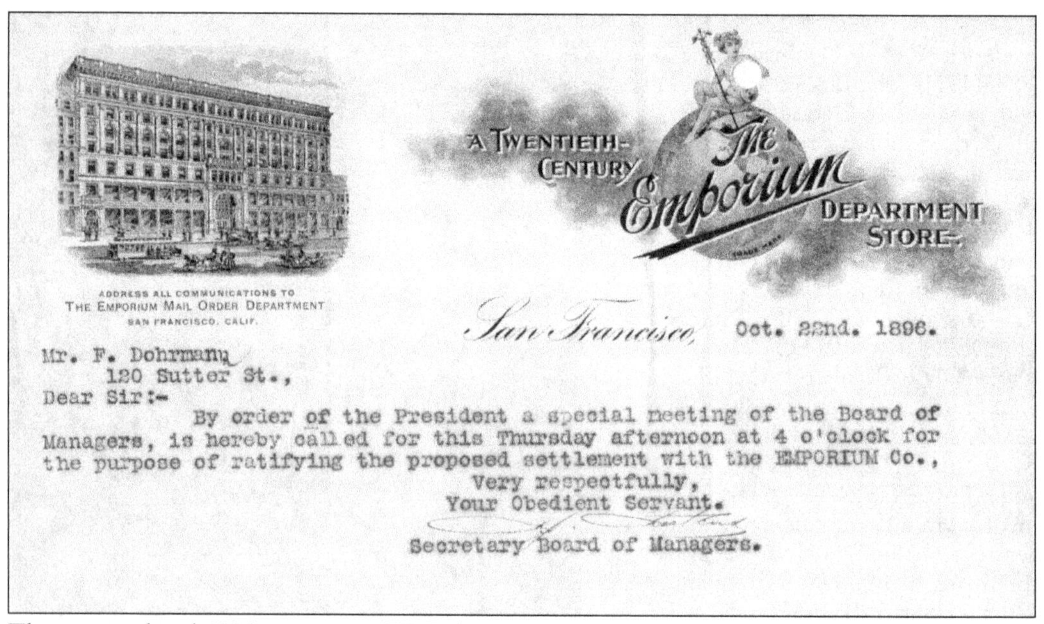

A TWENTIETH-CENTURY *The Emporium* DEPARTMENT STORE

ADDRESS ALL COMMUNICATIONS TO
THE EMPORIUM MAIL ORDER DEPARTMENT
SAN FRANCISCO, CALIF.

San Francisco, Oct. 22nd. 1896.

Mr. F. Dohrmann
120 Sutter St.,
Dear Sir:-
By order of the President a special meeting of the Board of Managers, is hereby called for this Thursday afternoon at 4 o'clock for the purpose of ratifying the proposed settlement with the EMPORIUM Co.,
Very respectfully,
Your Obedient Servant.
Secretary Board of Managers.

This memo dated 1896 summons F.W. Dohrmann to a meeting regarding the reorganization of the store, since the original Emporium had gone bankrupt. (Courtesy of the Bancroft Library, University of California, Berkeley, 91/29c ctn 1:1.)

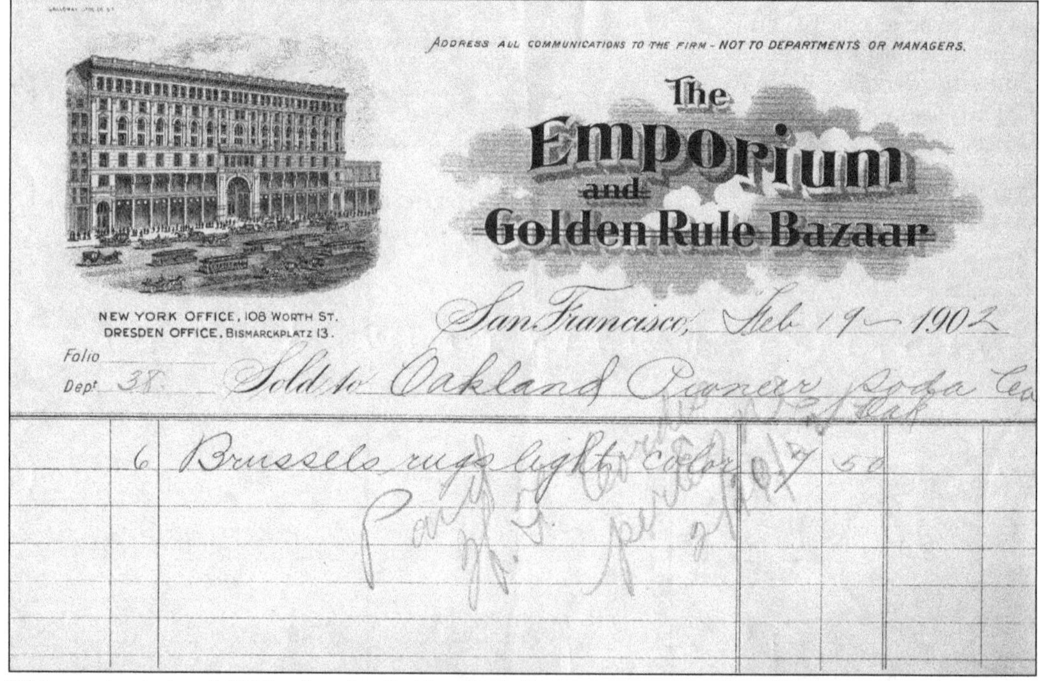

ADDRESS ALL COMMUNICATIONS TO THE FIRM - NOT TO DEPARTMENTS OR MANAGERS.

The Emporium and Golden Rule Bazaar

NEW YORK OFFICE, 108 WORTH ST.
DRESDEN OFFICE, BISMARCKPLATZ 13.

San Francisco, Feb 19 1902

Folio
Dept. 38 Sold to Oakland Pioneer Soda Co

6 Brussels rugs light color 7 50

Paid

This receipt is dated 1902, after the Golden Rule Bazaar name was officially dropped. Perhaps they were waiting for a new batch of forms with just the Emporium's name. In the meantime, red lines were drawn through the Golden Rule Bazaar name. (Courtesy of the Collection of the Oakland Museum of California, H91.50.25, The Emporium, Receipt, 1902; gift of Mrs. Judy Soden.)

On the first floor of the store in 1905, tables are filled with towels, fabric bolts, and "men's furnishings." Signs say "men's and youths' clothing," "men's hats," and "men's furnishing goods." Several electric lights are attached to the walls, as well as braces or pipes from the old gas lights. (Courtesy of the Collection of the Oakland Museum of California, H96.18.960, Gelatin silver, 8 x 10 in; gift of the Emporium.)

This is an image of one of the arcades, the "Oriental Section." As an 1896 *San Francisco Chronicle* article stated, "There is a department of Chinese curios, presided over by Chinese, and a Turkish department manned by embroidered and fezzed Turks." (Author's collection.)

This display case featured carpets from around the world. A 1909 Emporium ad offered "Genuine Oriental Rugs [that] will wear a lifetime." Consumers could find exotic "Karabagh, Shirvan, Mossoul, Kahistan, Khiva, Bokhara, Kelim, Kazak, Saruk, Tabriz, Gorevan, Serapi Kermanshah Ispahan and Meshhed in small sizes, hall strips and carpet size." (Courtesy of Louis Capecci.)

This display of the Emporium's sewing notions counter on the main floor shows stacks of ribbons and laces. Although ready-to-wear clothing became more available during World War I, there was still a great demand for fabrics and notions in the early part of the 20th century. Isaac Singer designed his first marketable sewing machine in 1850, and by 1889, Singer was marketing electric sewing machines for home use. (Courtesy of the Westfield San Francisco Centre.)

A woman peruses the many offerings on the selling floor in the jewelry department around 1898. The grand bandstand is on the left. In the days before self-service, salesmen stand waiting for her order. The young boys to her right could be "cash boys," whose job was to take cash that a customer paid for goods to the cashier's office. The cashier would then note the sale and give the boy the change to run back to the customer. Pneumatic tubes eventually replaced the cash boys. As far as the customers' jewelry selection, in the last decade of the 19th century, machine-made jewelry, which had once been welcomed as an innovation, was out of fashion. Jewelry designs were light and airy compared to the previous era of heavy jewels in dark colors. Women's jewels featured pierced filigrees, bows, ribbons and baskets, and pearls mixed with diamonds (or pastes). (Courtesy of Louis Capecci.)

NEXT WEDNESDAY SOLOIST NIGHT—CONCERT BEGINS AT 8 O'CLOCK.

Stocks Largest—Assortments Greatest—Prices Lowest

60 Departments

Ten times larger than any other Store in San Francisco and Grandest in the World

Goods Sold for Cash only—Money Cheerfully Refunded

Send for Catalogue

The Emporium

SAN FRANCISCO, Sept. 27, 1896.

Women's Outer Garments.

Enticing Bargains in Black and Colored Dress Goods, Velvets, Silks, Blankets and Comforts.

Opening Sale Fur Garments.

Dress Goods Bargain Carnival.

September Silk Sale.

Fur Cape Special.

Colored Dress Goods.

Winter Blankets.

Black Dress Goods.

Warmer Underwear For Men.

PICTURE AND FRAME DEPARTMENT.

Comfort Specials.

Velvets as Never Before.

Artists' Materials.

FALL STYLES FOR FEET.

By far the largest assortment of Shoes in San Francisco. Peerless in style, quality and low prices. Here are six very Special Bargains for Men, Women and Children.

CROCKERY SPECIALS.

Men's Fall Derbys $2.00.

This Dinner Set - $5.40

Free for The Asking.

"Ten times larger than any other store in San Francisco and Grandest in the World" reads this 1896 ad. That might be a bit of an exaggeration, but it illustrates how the store positioned itself to its customers and drew them to the Market Street location. (Courtesy of the Library of Congress, Chronicling America.)

THE SAN FRANCISCO CALL, WEDNESDAY,

EMPORIUM MANAGEMENT ENTERTAINS EMPLOYES

The Emporium, known for treating its employees fairly, held annual balls under the dome for all employees, with management in attendance. According to an 1896 article in the *San Francisco Call*, "The music for the first dance was sounded at 9 o'clock, and from that time on till after midnight, when the last of eighteen numbers had been stepped off, the merriest time imaginable was had, with pleasant intermissions for little bites and many opportunities for little têtes-à-têtes." (Courtesy of the Library of Congress, Chronicling America.)

The concerts "under the Dome" were a big draw. In the newspaper ad at right, the store promotes a three-hour Grand Matinee Concert, with a list of the 21 musical compositions being offered that afternoon. The store also provided a trained nurse who oversaw an emergency hospital and a children's nursery. Mothers could leave their "little boys in the barber-shop to have their hair cut while they are shopping in other parts of the building." The image on the urn below shows the Emporium interior with the bandstand and dome. (Right, courtesy of the Library of Congress, Chronicling America; below, courtesy of Harold Rudolph.)

THE EMPORIUM. | THE EMPORIUM. | THE EMPORIUM.

The Cafe under the great dome is a delightful place to lunch in while shopping in the EMPORIUM.

A trained nurse from the Waldeck Sanitarium in charge of the emergency hospital and children's nursery.

Concerts this week Wednesday afternoon and Saturday night only.

We have the exclusive agency in San Francisco for the genuine JOUVIN & CIE Kid Gloves—the best in the world.

Mothers find it very convenient to leave their little boys in the barber-shop to have their hair cut while they are shopping in other parts of the building.

Address all mail order communications to the "Mail Order Department," THE EMPORIUM.

GRAND MATINEE CONCERT WEDNESDAY AFTERNOON.

2 to 5 O'Clock—See the Program Below.

WASH FABRICS AND LINENS TO-DAY

WASH FABRIC SELLING.

The weeks go rapidly by. Vacation begins next Saturday. Are you ready with all your Summer Dresses? Are the children all fitted out for the mountains and seashore? If not, an opportunity awaits you to-day to buy the proper kind of Wash Materials at much less than their proper prices.

THE LINEN SELLING.

Direct from Ireland and Austria to America. Direct from the manufacturers to the EMPORIUM. Only one profit to pay on your Linens at the EMPORIUM at all times—less than one profit to-day.

Program, Wednesday, June 17, 2 P. M.

PART I.

PART II.

BOYS' AND MEN'S HATS.

Do You Need a Good Clock
Here's a $6.50 One for $2.60.

HOSIERY SPECIALS.

These are the lowest prices for HOSIERY that have ever been made in San Francisco. Make an examination of the goods and see for yourself whether you have ever been able to buy similar qualities for similar prices.

MEN'S SUITS, $12.45.

CHILDREN'S HOSE.

BOYS' SUITS, $1.85.

LADIES' HOSE.

This Handsome New Upright Piano, with stool and cover, $165.

BOYS' WASH SUITS, $1.35

BOYS' WAISTS, 20c EACH.

THE EMPORIUM, SAN FRANCISCO.

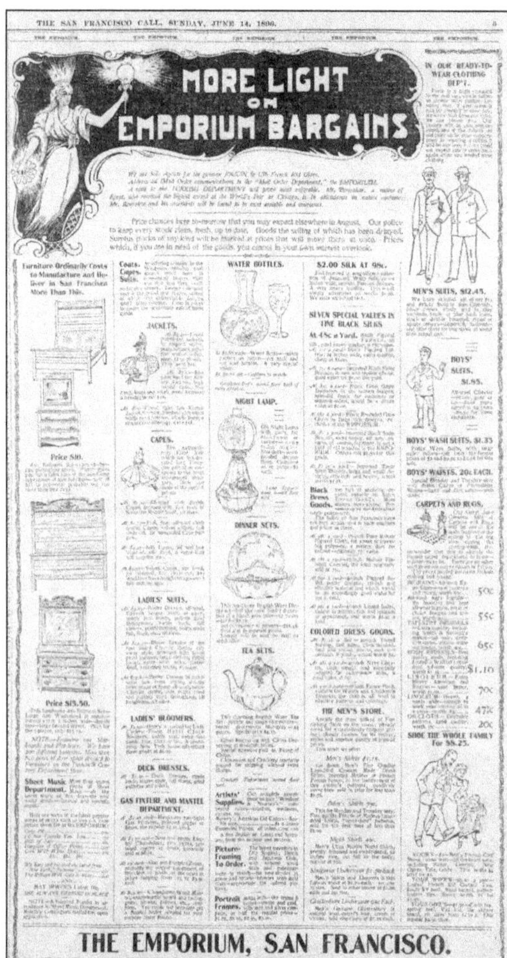
THE SAN FRANCISCO CALL, SUNDAY, JUNE 14, 1896.

MORE LIGHT ON EMPORIUM BARGAINS

THE EMPORIUM, SAN FRANCISCO.

The Emporium prided itself on customer service. In this ad for their ready-to wear clothing line for men and boys, they claimed, "Our clothes will fit you, rest assured, and if the fabrics do not come up to your expectation in wearing qualities, it will be our loss, for we could not expect you to come back again when you needed more clothing." (Courtesy of the Library of Congress, Chronicling America.)

THE RAINY DAY SHOPPING PLACE—ALL CLASSES OF MERCHANDISE UNDER ONE ROOF.

The Emporium.

SAN FRANCISCO, Dec. 30, 1896.

A FEW WORDS ABOUT STOVES

We never told you about our Stoves. Of course the EMPORIUM sells Stoves. We sell everything that man, woman or child can eat, wear or use in their houses. We believe that we have the best line of Stoves and Ranges west of Chicago—and there are none better there—they cannot be made better. We are not only in a position to offer you a superior article, but

WE CAN SAVE YOU SOME MONEY.

Our Grand, Superior No. 8 Stove consumes very little coal, is a fine baker, has six holes, a large oven, an ideal stove for a large family. OUR price......**$32.00**
Put up anywhere in the city with stove pipes and hot-water connections for $37.50.

The picture shows our Grand, Superior No. 7 Stove, chilled iron grate, six holes, large oven. Our price for this Stove is

$29.00

High shelf, like picture, $4 extra.

Put up complete without high shelf, but including stove pipes and hot-water connections, for $34.

Our Grand, Superior No. 7, with six holes, a plain cooking stove, reliable in every way, for........**$26.50**

No. 8 Ivy Cooking Stove, with six holes, a well-known and popular make. EMPORIUM price........**$23.00**

No. 7 Ruby Cooking Stove, six holes; as good a one would cost you in any other store $20. EMPORIUM price........**$16.00**

We are also selling agents for the Celebrated Welcome Universal Stoves. OUR prices for these are:

No. 8 Universal Cooking Stove - $25 | No. 7 Universal Cooking Stove - $20
No. 7 Prize Universal Cooking Stove - $15.50

. . . .HERE'S A SPECIAL. . . .

The EMPORIUM No. 7 Cooking Stove, five holes on top, good sized oven, a small consumer of coal, a good baker. At the special price of........**$13.00**
We will put up and connect the same with water box, pipes and elbows, complete and ready for use, for $18.

House Furnishing Goods Department, Basement.

With over 60 different departments, the Emporium promoted itself as "The Rainy Day Shopping Place" in this ad for stoves, stating, "We sell everything that man, woman or child can eat, wear or use in their houses." They also offered installation, or "put up," for a fee. (Courtesy of the Library of Congress, Chronicling America.)

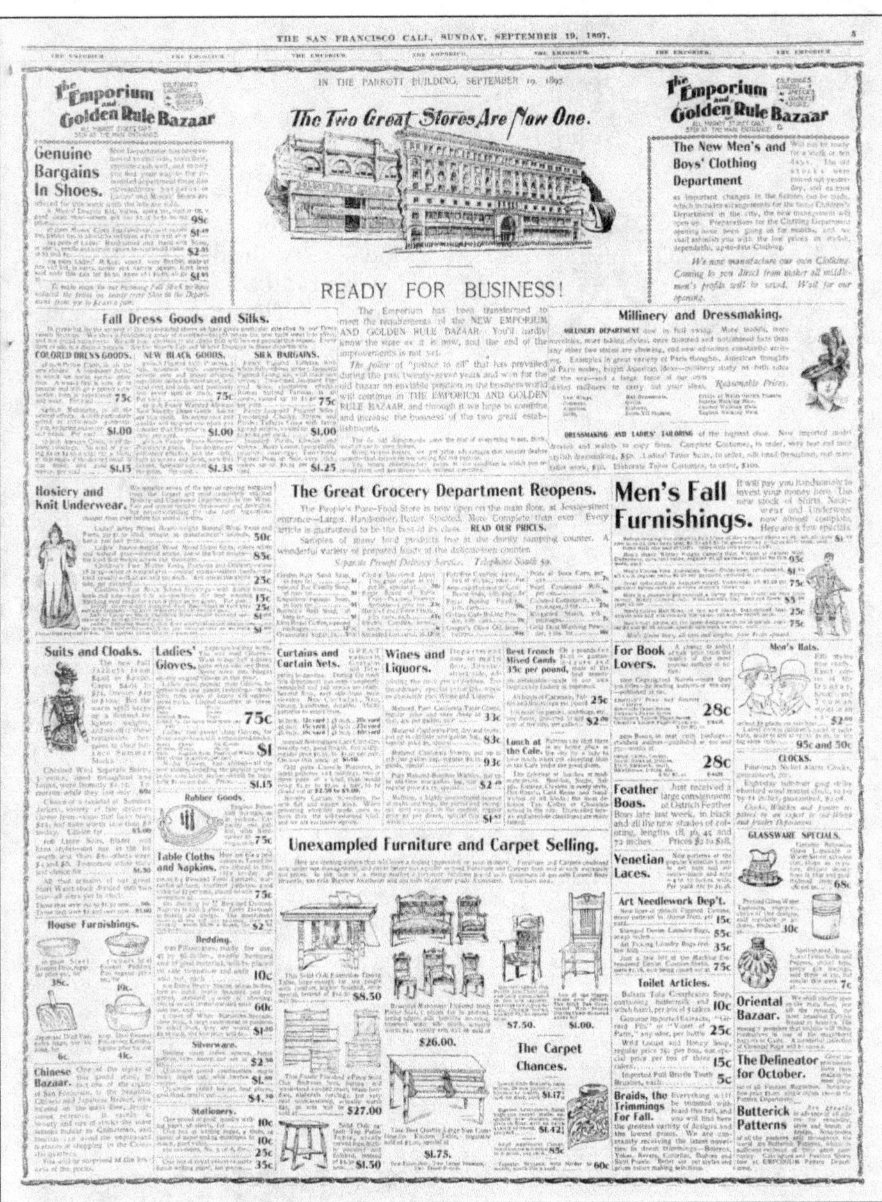

THE SAN FRANCISCO CALL, SUNDAY, SEPTEMBER 19, 1897.

IN THE PARROTT BUILDING, SEPTEMBER 19, 1897

The Emporium and Golden Rule Bazaar

The Two Great Stores Are Now One.

READY FOR BUSINESS!

Genuine Bargains In Shoes.

The New Men's and Boys' Clothing Department

Fall Dress Goods and Silks.

COLORED DRESS GOODS. NEW BLACK GOODS. SILK BARGAINS.

Millinery and Dressmaking.

Hosiery and Knit Underwear.

The Great Grocery Department Reopens.

Men's Fall Furnishings.

Suits and Cloaks.

Ladies' Gloves.

Curtains and Curtain Nets.

Wines and Liquors.

Best French Mixed Candy 35c per pound.

For Book Lovers.

Men's Hats.

Rubber Goods.

Table Cloths and Napkins.

House Furnishings.

Bedding.

Silverware.

Stationery.

Chinese Bazaar.

Unexampled Furniture and Carpet Selling.

$8.50

$26.00.

$27.00

$1.75.

$1.50

$7.50.

$1.00.

The Carpet Chances.

Feather Boas.

Venetian Laces.

GLASSWARE SPECIALS.

CLOCKS.

Art Needlework Dep't.

Toilet Articles.

Oriental Bazaar.

The Delineator for October.

Braids, the Trimmings For Fall.

Butterick Patterns

"The Two Great Stores are Now One!" This newspaper ad from September 1897 announces the merger of the Emporium and the Golden Rule Bazaar. The ad declares, "The 60-odd departments carry the best of everything to eat, drink, wear or use in your homes." The store positioned itself to attract value-oriented shoppers, saying, "Being largest buyers, we get price advantages that smaller dealers cannot—that means money-saving for our patrons." The Golden Rule Bazaar brought with it goodwill and tradition, and the combined stores became one of the city's most popular institutions. F.W. Dohrmann, in a memo outlining the goals of the newly formed organization, wrote, "The right example of the leaders will determine the action of subordinates, and the spirit, the honor, the strict integrity, the goods and honored name of the house will in time become more valuable, and be a better inheritance to those to whom we leave our early possessions when our time comes, than mere gains and riches, and will besides be the best and cheapest advertising we can possibly do." (Courtesy of the Library of Congress, Chronicling America.)

Sears, Roebuck & Co. led the way with its first mail-order catalog, advertising watches and jewelry, in 1888. Thanks to volume buying, railroads, post offices, and later, rural free delivery and parcel post, mail-order catalogs offered a welcome alternative to high-priced stores. By 1894, the Sears catalog had grown to 322 pages, featuring sewing machines, bicycles, sporting goods, and a host of other new items. By the following year, Sears added dolls, iceboxes, cook stoves, and groceries to the catalog. Never one to miss an advertising opportunity, the Emporium produced its own mail-order catalog, *The Emporium Economist*. Even though this 1905–1906 edition was only 138 pages, compared to Sears's 300-plus pages, it included everything from furniture to clothing to flags. (Both courtesy of Ron Ross.)

In the early 1900s, the fashion was the "Gibson Girl" hairstyle, with masses of wavy hair swept up to the top of the head and gathered into a knot. Here, the Emporium advertises the fashionable large broad-brimmed hats, trimmed with masses of feathers, decorated with ribbons and artificial flowers, and occasionally complete with stuffed birds. (Courtesy of Ron Ross.)

For men, the mail-order catalog offered coats, waistcoats, and trousers. In the early 1900s, men wore three-piece suits, consisting of a sack coat with matching vest and trousers. Trousers often had turn-ups or cuffs, and they were creased in front and back using the new trouser press. Waistcoats were fastened high on the chest. The usual style was single-breasted. (Courtesy of Ron Ross.)

14 FALL The Emporium WINTER

Children's and Misses' Coats and Dresses

In the early 1900s, girls' fashion imitated women's, although girls' dresses only went to knee length, with lace and embroidery trimmings at the hem. Black shoes or button-up or lace-up boots and woolen stockings completed the look, as well as kid leather or crochet gloves. Girls' hair was generally worn long and curly, with a ribbon for decoration. Boys often wore sailor suits, consisting of a shirt with a sailor collar and trousers or knickerbockers. Boys got to look more sporty when they went for a ride in automobiles; the fashionable lad wore a duster with knickerbockers, a flat cap, and goggles. (Both courtesy of Ron Ross.)

SAN FRANCISCO The Emporium CALIFORNIA 15

INFANTS' AND CHILDREN'S COATS AND CAPS

No. 1501. Infants' silk cap, embroidered and with full front ruche, sizes 12 to 15, like cut. **35c.**

No. 1503. Silk cap, silk strings and lining, heavily embroidered full face ruche, all sizes, **50c.**

No. 1505. Cream silk cap, dainty embroidery design, flat front, lace trimmed, all sizes. **75c.**

No. 1506. Bengaline silk cap, baby ribbon rosettes, chiffon ruching, all sizes, **75c.**

No. 1509. Silk embroidered cap, silk lining and strings, Dutch effect, ribbosene rosette and ends, all sizes, **98c.**

No. 1511. Bengaline poke bonnet in cream, red or navy, lace edging in front, sizes 14 to 17, **75c.**

No. 1513. Silk poke, shirred front, liberty silk ruching in sizes 14, 15 and 16. In red, navy or cream. Price, **$1.25.**

No. 1515. Bengaline silk poke, braid trimmed full ribbon rosettes, chiffon ruching, dainty tie in red, navy or cream, sizes 14, 15 and 16. Price, **$2.00.**

No. 1517. Bengaline silk poke full double plaited front, ribbon trimmed, silk lining, wide ties, in red, navy, cream, sizes 14, 15 and 16. Price, **$2.50.**

No. 1519. Cream Bedford cord coat in long lengths 1 and 2 years, full collar cord trimmed with ribbon, insertion effect, **$1.75.**

No. 1521. Cream Bedford cord coat in long lengths 1 and 2 years, fancy braid and ribbon trimmed, like cut **$2.50.**

No. 1523. Cream Bedford coat in 1 and 2 year sizes, octagon shaped collar, six rows of fancy braid, **$3.00.**

No. 1525. Colored flannel coats in red, navy, tan or brown, round collar, white braid trimmed, sacque back, sizes 2, 4, 6 years, **$2.50.**

No. 1527. Bedford cord coat in all wool material, Russian effect, kid belt, embroidered scallops, in cream, tan, light blue or red, sizes 2, 4 and 6 years, **$5.00.**

No. 1529. Crushed plush coats in red, navy, green or brown, trimmed in French knots and pipings of contrasting colors and six large white pearl buttons, strapped back, sizes 2, 4 and 6 years. Price, **$6.00.**

Two

1906–1908
The Earthquake and its Aftermath

Everything changed on April 18, 1906. The earthquake was powerful (around 7.9), but it was the subsequent out-of-control fires that caused the most damage. Over 30 fires destroyed approximately 25,000 buildings on almost 500 city blocks.

The Emporium, and most of Market Street, was devastated. Only the Emporium's front and dome survived. Store management immediately set about finding temporary quarters for the store, which managed to reopen in May 1906 in the Hecht residence at Van Ness Avenue and Post Street. They also built another building surrounding the original residence, and then an annex in the rear. Finally, they completed a two-story building with 70 feet of frontage on Sutter Street.

The store not only survived; it prospered. Henry Dernham, the general manager, said in the *San Francisco Chronicle* on July 29, 1906, that the sales volume was far greater than he had expected or dared to hope for, and "it seemed as though the only limit was in the ability of Emporium buyers to secure merchandise and in acquiring sufficient space in which to handle both goods and customers."

F.W. Dohrmann, the store's president, was in Europe that April, but he returned immediately and became active in the rehabilitation of the city. He served on the finance committee, which handled the Red Cross funds. Mayor Eugene Schmitz appointed one of F.W.'s sons, A.B.C. Dohrmann, to be on the Committee of Fifty, which was comprised of civic leaders, entrepreneurs, newspaper men, and politicians, to manage the crisis.

At first, European insurance companies refused to pay claims for fire damage for many San Francisco policyholders, believing that it was the quake that caused the damage (they did not insure against earthquakes). In November 1906, F.W. Dohrmann, together with Oscar Sutro and William Thomas, went to Europe to negotiate with the insurance companies. They were instrumental in considerably increasing the insurance companies' payouts. As evidence, Dohrmann and the others took with them hundreds of photographs showing San Francisco before and after the earthquake, and then after the fire.

The Emporium operated in its temporary buildings until October 1908, when a rebuilt Emporium on Market Street opened to great fanfare.

ENTIRE CITY OF SAN FRANCISCO IN DANGER OF BEING ANNIHILATED

Big Business Buildings Already Consumed by Fire and Dynamite---30,000 Smaller Structures Swept Out and Remainder Are Doomed

PANIC-STRICKEN PEOPLE FLEE

750 ARE TREATED

DEAD IN STREET

BIG FIRE IN MISSION

SAN FRANCISCO, April 18. —A great fire is raging in the Mission district and is utterly beyond control. Before night, it is estimated, that in this particular section of the city 30,000 persons will be homeless.

RESIDENCES BURNING

SAN FRANCISCO, April 18. —An intense fire broke out late this afternoon immediately west of the Mechanics' Pavilion, threatening to destroy one of the most thickly populated residence districts of the city. As there were no fire apparatus on hand the flames are raging unchecked.

RUINS 20 COMPANIES

EMPORIUM IN RUINS

SAN FRANCISCO, April 18. —The Emporium is a mass of ruins, with nothing but the walls of this magnificent store standing. The buildings immediately adjoining it are doomed to destruction.

DYNAMITE BUILDINGS

SAN FRANCISCO, April 18. —At 2:30 o'clock this afternoon the firemen are dynamiting one of the most imposing structures on Market street. Buildings in the vicinity of the United States Mint and the United States Postoffice were blown up in the hope that they would be saved. Both of them are in grave danger, and while standing the shock of the earthquake, will probably fall victims of the uncontrollable conflagration raging in that vicinity.

DOCTOR'S BRAVERY

FATEFUL BUILDING

WITHOUT A NEWSPAPER

DAMAGE A BILLION

THEATERS RUINED

All of San Francisco's best playhouses, including the Majestic, Columbia and Grand Opera House, are a mass of ruins. The earthquake demolished them for all practical purposes, and at the present time it appears the fire will complete the work of demolition. The Rialto and Caswerly buildings were burned to the ground, as was everything in that district.

The Terminal Hotel at the foot of Market street fell this morning and buried twenty persons under the debris. These were incinerated, and there is no possibility of learning their identity.

NARROW ESCAPE

"Emporium in Ruins" declared the *San Francisco Call* on April 19, 1906, the day after the earthquake. Newspapers all over the country were carrying the story of the great earthquake and fire that threatened to destroy the entire city of San Francisco. Reporters hurried from one scene to another. The fire burned continuously during Wednesday and Thursday (when its main progress was checked), and to a small extent on Friday and Saturday. "The Emporium is a mass of ruins, with nothing but the walls of this magnificent store standing. The buildings immediately adjoining it are doomed to destruction." In the histrionic tone typical of the era, the newspaper said that total annihilation seemed to be San Francisco's fate, and that "indescribable confusion" and "indescribable madness" reigned. "Thrilling rescues" and "deeds of valor would fill a volume." (Courtesy of the Library of Congress, Chronicling America.)

Water mains had ruptured, so the San Francisco Fire Department (SFFD) had little access to water. The city's fire chief, Dennis T. Sullivan, was seriously injured when the earthquake first struck, later dying from his injuries. The interim fire chief sent an urgent request to the Presidio, the Army post on the edge of the city, for dynamite to demolish buildings in order to create firebreaks they hoped would contain the flames. Members of the SFFD and the troops who helped them had virtually no experience with using dynamite to fight fire. To make matters worse, the Presidio sent the incorrect type of explosive: highly flammable black gunpowder, which was not as effective as nitroglycerine, stick dynamite, or gun cotton. (Both courtesy of the Library of Congress.)

After the quake struck in the early morning, the fire department responded to 52 fire alarms in the first half hour. The fires continued to burn for three days and three nights and were more catastrophic than the earthquake itself. As Charles B. Sedgwick, an eyewitness and the editor of the *British-Californian*, noted, "That night I climbed to the summit of Russian Hill to view the conflagration, and never shall I forget the sight. It was weirdly beautiful. A thousand banners of

flame were streaming in the cloudless sky from spires and domes and lofty roofs . . . magnificent in irresistible power . . . towering buildings, eaten loose, toppled and fell, or were lifted skyward by thundering dynamite, to then scatter and drop, throwing up huge fiery splashes from the burning sea." (Author's collection.)

These are two views of the smoldering ruins of the Emporium. Although the dome fell and was damaged, it survived along with the brick and sandstone facade. Together with quantities of merchandise, records, and equipment, the rest of the building had been destroyed. An internal Emporium memo about the earthquake declared, "To see the Emporium facade standing intact amid the surrounding ruins was a very reassuring sight, a symbol of strength to San Francisco, for it represented not merely the front wall of a store, but the entrance to a beloved institution through whose doors had passed thousands of people for pleasure as well as for purchases." (Both photographs by Bear Photograph Co.; courtesy of the California History Room, California State Library, Sacramento, California.)

Although the newspaper headlines described widespread panic, Charles B. Sedgwick, the editor of the *British-Californian*, remarked, "There was no excitement, no confusion, no panic. Neither was there any fear, any terror, any grief . . . none of these scenes figured in San Francisco's fall. People were much about the same as usual. Men and women came down town to see what was going on, gazed about in blank astonishment for a few moments, then stood idly by, or went their way as though nothing extraordinary was transpiring. It was this indifference, or philosophical resignation to the inevitable, that struck me as the most marvelous thing in connection with the great tragedy." (Right, photograph by Bear Photograph Co.; below, photograph by Albert Dressler; both courtesy of the California History Room, California State Library, Sacramento, California.)

As the earthquake rocked the city, hundreds of buildings south of Market Street were either thrown down or badly shattered. In the ensuing inferno, the entire district south of Mission was a mass of fire, which leapt from block to block. The fire swept up Fifth Street, destroying buildings like the Emporium and sending bursts of flame hundreds of feet into the air. As Frank W. Aitken and Edward Hilton wrote in their book *History of the Earthquake and Fire in San Francisco*, people never "thought that the fire department would be unequal to its task. Never before had it failed to handle every fire that occurred; always it had protected them and their wooden city from the greedy flames." (Above, photograph by Albert Dressler, courtesy of the California History Room, California State Library, Sacramento, California; below, author's collection.)

Squads of dynamiters set charges, and with a roar and a cloud of dust, a building would fall. Unfortunately, many charges were set by unskilled hands, and the fire was scattered. The chief operator of the postal telegraph office on Market Street sent out this message, "Destruction by earthquake something frightful. The City Hall dome stripped and only the frame work standing . . . The Emporium is gone, entire building, also the Old Flood Building. Lots of new buildings just recently finished are completely destroyed. They are blowing standing buildings that are in the path of flames up with dynamite. No water. It's awful. There is no communication anywhere and entire phone system is busted. I want to get out of here or [I will] be blown up." (Right, courtesy of Pam Gibson; below, courtesy of the National Archives.)

The town was under martial law. Mayor Eugene Schmitz proclaimed, "The Federal Troops, the members of the Regular Police Force, and all Special Police Officers have been authorized by me to KILL any and all persons found engaged in Looting or in the Commission of Any Other Crime. I have directed all the Gas and Electric Lighting Companies not to turn on Gas or Electricity until I order them to do so. You may therefore expect the city to remain in darkness for an indefinite time. I request all citizens to remain at home from darkness until daylight every night until order is restored. I WARN all Citizens of the danger of fire from Damaged or Destroyed Chimneys, Broken or Leaking Gas Pipes or Fixtures, or any like cause." (Above, photograph by Arnold Genthe, courtesy of the Library of Congress, Chronicling America; below, courtesy of the National Archives.)

After the shock shattered the principal water mains, the fire department was practically helpless. Overturned stoves, electric wires, and gas leaks fueled the fire. The firemen turned on their hose. There was one rush of water; then the flow stopped. The water main, which carried the city's chief water supply, ran through the ruined district. It had been broken, and the useless water was spurting up through the ruins in scores of places. Meanwhile, thieves burgled wrecked stores and deserted homes, and rowdies broke into saloons and helped themselves to liquor. Troops began patrolling the streets, and Mayor Schmitz issued his "shoot to kill" order. (Both photographs by Detroit Publishing Co.; courtesy of the Library of Congress.)

Again, from eyewitness Charles Sedgwick, observing the earthquake's aftermath on Market Street, "Now the grand old street was scarcely recognizable—a sad scene of destruction. Buildings by the dozen were half down; great pillars, copings, cornices and ornamentations had been wrenched from the mightiest structures and dashed to the ground in fragments; the huge store windows had been shattered and costly displays of goods were with much litter on the floors . . . The massive Emporium frontage was scarred in a dozen places." (Left, author's collection; below, photograph by Underwood & Underwood, 1906, courtesy of the California History Room, California State Library, Sacramento, California.)

All of the Emporium's records were destroyed or lost, with the exception of the accounts payable, which showed how much the store owed, but not how much was owed to it. In order to collect their outstanding bills, the store advertised in the newspapers inviting customers to pay what they owed. It is a tribute to the loyalty of its customers that many customers voluntarily paid their bills, even though there was no written record of transactions. What records were salvaged were mailed to the store by the US post office, because several quick-thinking employees had stuffed the records in a US mail bag before fleeing the fire. The mail bags were dumped on Jessie Street and forgotten. A mail carrier passing by saw them, and, thinking them to be mail, rescued them. (Right, courtesy of the San Francisco History Center, San Francisco Public Library; below, author's collection.)

This interior shot of the Emporium shows the extent of the destruction. In the *Argonaut*, a weekly newspaper, the writer's description of the destruction of city hall is also apt for what happened to the Emporium: "In the space of a minute a building that was architecturally the largest and most pretentious in the State of California was shaken to the ground almost like a pack of cards." The Parrott Building's first and second floors, occupied by the Emporium, were intended to be fireproof. The floor arches were of hollow tile, and the columns were encased in the same material. Above the third floor (there were seven stories in front and five in the wings and rear), the floors and their supports, and most of the partitions, were of wood. The great quantities of flammable merchandise caught fire. Most of the store's destruction was due to the fire, not the quake. (Courtesy of the San Francisco History Center, San Francisco Public Library.)

This photograph shows meal time in Union Square, a block from the Emporium, in the Mrs. W.H. Crocker Camp. William Henry Crocker, a financier, was president of Crocker Bank. To accommodate the thousands of people left homeless, the Army ran 21 official refugee camps in vacant lots and parks and open spaces, where they distributed food, clothing, and other necessities to quake victims. Among themselves, the campers established their own disciplinary governments. They chose leaders and established regulations for the conduct and sanitation of the camps, which had to be obeyed at peril of expulsion from the camp. Later, these governments were merged into the general relief organization. The San Francisco Red Cross and Relief Corporation and the Army were administrators. Emporium president F.W. Dohrmann was on the finance committee, which handled the Red Cross funds, and afterwards was chairman of the board of trustees of the Red Cross. (Photograph by Bear Photograph Co.; courtesy of the California History Room, California State Library, Sacramento, California.)

The Emporium set up its temporary headquarters (left) on Van Ness Avenue, a north-south thoroughfare running from Market Street north to the bay. Prior to the earthquake, it was a quiet residential neighborhood of mansions, but the Army used the street as a firebreak after the earthquake. Many of the buildings along the street were dynamited in an ultimately successful attempt to keep the firestorm from spreading west to the entire city. Following the quake, Van Ness served as the temporary commercial center and main thoroughfare of the city. (Both photographs by Albert Dressler; courtesy of the California History Room, California State Library, Sacramento, California.)

The Emporium commenced business in a residence owned by one of its stockholders, Elias Hecht. One of the bathrooms served as the business office, and the employment office was in the clothes closet. The entire house was used, including the stable and hot house, as well as an annex that was built in the rear. The two-story building ended up having almost as much selling space as on Market Street, making their salesroom again the largest on the West Coast, if not the largest west of Chicago. F.S. "Daddy" Owles, who was then the New York office head, sent carloads of merchandise immediately, so the Emporium was the first department store to reopen after the fire. This speedy delivery of merchandise was a real inspiration to the revival of trade in San Francisco. (Above, courtesy of Pam Gibson; below, courtesy of Louis Capecci.)

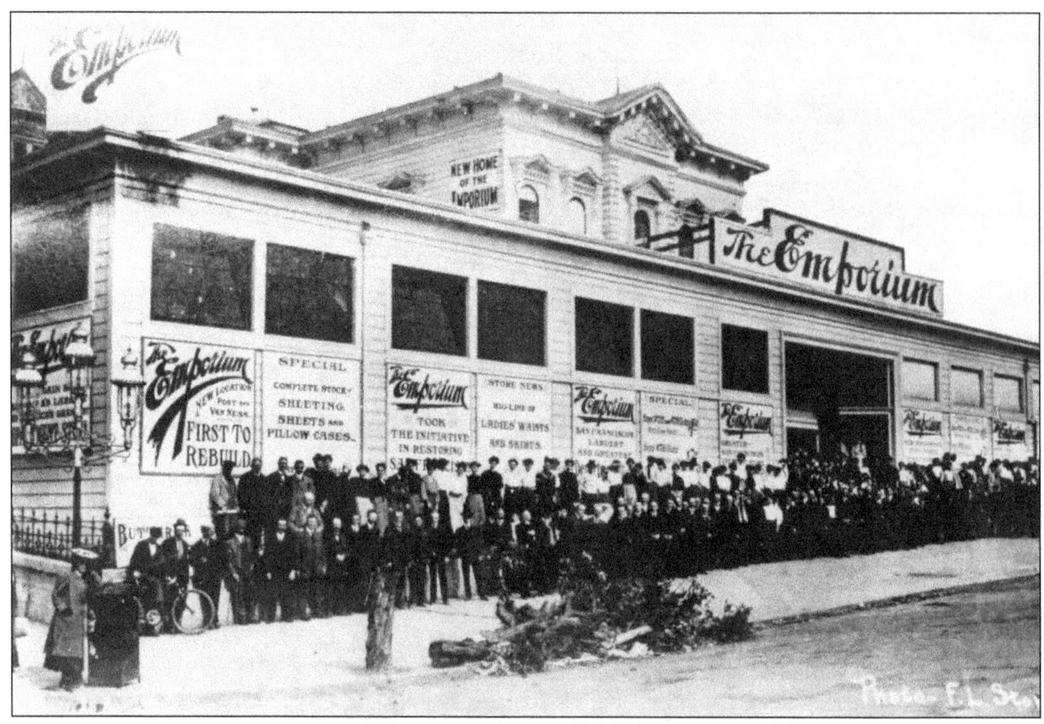

The Emporium lost no time in starting reconstruction. The photograph above shows the temporary store on Van Ness Avenue with lines waiting to get in. The photograph below shows crews in 1907 working on the new store, which opened in late 1908. In envisioning its new store, the company made a special effort to include all the latest ideas in department store construction and arrangement. One manager went to Europe to visit all the "principal cities of the Continent," according to the *San Francisco Chronicle* of April 14, 1907, in search of new ideas. General manager Henry Dernham went east to study large department stores there. They endeavored to "take the best from each place that they visit." The Emporium reopened with another stunning skylight, a reconstructed 500,000-pound, 102-foot-wide dome, 775,000 square feet of floor space, a glass arcade, solid mahogany fixtures, and a new grocery department. San Francisco's rebuilt store was as grand and elegant as anything on the East Coast. (Above, courtesy of Pam Gibson; below, courtesy of the San Francisco History Center, San Francisco Public Library.)

Three

1908–1919
Glory Days

The city was quickly rebuilt, and it soon looked cleaner and more modern. The fire had destroyed the slums south of Market, and the old Victorian downtown was gone. Within weeks, streetcars were running on Market Street. By July, the *Chronicle* was back in its former headquarters. By August, the California Street Cable Railroad Co. repaired its powerhouse, put the cable machinery back in order, and was running cable cars to the top of Nob Hill again.

When the Emporium reopened on October 1, 1908, the store invited the public to come through the portals of the past (the original doors) into the store of the present. It was built along the same lines as the original, but on a much grander scale. At first, two floors were sufficient selling space, with the others leased to offices. As business boomed, however, the store expanded rapidly. The Basement Salesroom, which opened in 1911, covered 40,000 square feet, and sold lower-priced goods drawn from every department in the house, with the exception of the men's clothing department. The store soon expanded to other floors, and even had an auditorium on the third floor with a seating capacity of 500 people. As a May 21, 1916, *San Francisco Chronicle* article stated, "The question is not 'What can I buy?', but 'What can't I buy?' " The store stayed open until there were no more customers to wait on.

In 1915, with war already raging in Europe, the city hosted the Panama-Pacific Exposition, officially to celebrate the opening of the Panama Canal, but also to showcase the completely rebuilt city less than a decade after the earthquake. The Emporium was gaily bedecked to welcome exposition visitors.

By 1918, America was involved in World War I, but, despite the demands of wartime, the Emporium opened a nine-story annex building. The new "service annex" included employees' quarters, recreation rooms, a roof garden, children's playgrounds, a library, medical and dental quarters, cafés, a billiard room, and offices. Many Emporium employees served in the war, and the store held events for the Red Cross, Liberty Loans, and the Food Conservation program, which included Victory gardens, "wheatless Wednesdays," and "meatless Mondays."

From the time the Emporium reopened after the earthquake until 1929, the year of the stock market crash, consumer demand skyrocketed, roughly tripling. The Emporium's beautiful new store was well positioned to take advantage of this demand, with its central location on Market Street in the newly rebuilt downtown. Americans were moving from rural to urban centers, and over 23 million immigrants came to the country during those years. These urban dwellers had an almost insatiable desire to move up, and the Emporium aimed not only to provide basic necessities, but also to satisfy all retail needs while providing entertainment and cultural outings. (Both, author's collection.)

These two views (above in 1909, and below in 1912) are looking down Market Street, with the Emporium ("California's Largest, America's Grandest, Store") on the right, the Flood Building on the left (above), and the Humboldt Bank and the Call Building, San Francisco's first skyscraper, behind. The Call Building, located at 703 Market Street, at the corner of Third Street, stood 310 feet tall and measured 75 feet on each side. The tower rose vertically for 15 stories, topped by a dome housing the 16th through 18th floors. Although badly damaged during the 1906 fire (a fireball blasted up floor by floor through the elevator shafts until it exited the dome), the Call Building remained structurally sound and was able to be refurbished rather than rebuilt. (Both, author's collection.)

This image from 1909 looks west down Market Street from Fourth Street. The Emporium is the building with the flags on the right. The large building in the foreground is the Pacific Building. Market Street post-earthquake continued to be a transit hub. Electric streetcars, which arrived around 1900, were taking the place of cable cars in some areas. The streetcars were more practical on most of the grades in hilly San Francisco, but, with their high capital costs, their development was slow. Much political maneuvering and public outcry ensued after all but three of the remaining independent railways consolidated into a monopolistic enterprise in 1902. Voters approved bond measures to create a municipal streetcar line in 1909. (Author's collection.)

These portraits, although not identified, are probably the managers or buyers for the various departments in the store. In a 1913 memo, F.W. Dohrmann stated that "justice tempered with kindness" was the way to treat employees. The employees should know that "they are going to have a fair deal and candid recognition of good service, and the best compensation and advancement that there is to give them." (Courtesy of Ron Ross.)

SECOND NEWS SECTION

THE CALL

SPORTING AUTOS SHIPPING

MILLION LIGHTS GREET TEMPLARS AT CONVENTION

BRILLIANT DISPLAY IN ILLUMINATIONS

The Emporium Graduates a Large Class

Vocational Training Proves to Be Success

Twenty-three Young Women Complete Study Of Best Methods of Selling Goods

IMPEACHMENT OF GOV. SULZER MAY BE ATTEMPTED

CHURCH DEACONS IN LEGAL DISPUTE

WILL FILED FOR PROBATE LEAVES RELATIVES OUT

PROF. CARRUTH OF K. U. ON STAFF OF STANFORD

DISTRICT ATTORNEY CITED BY JUDGE

ONLY 40 SPECTATORS TO SEE DIGGS CASE TRIED

MECHANICS FAIR TO BE TYPICALLY CALIFORNIAN

PHOENIX CLUB ROW MENACES LICENSE

JEWISH ASSEMBLY TO MEET FRIDAY

PORTERVILLE BUSINESS SECTION PARTLY BURNED

H. Liebes & Co. FURS

Our Mid-Summer Sale of FURS Is Now Going On

1/4 to 1/2 Off Marked Prices

COATS, SCARFS and MUFFS

REMEMBER

Remodeling and Repairing

H. Liebes & Co. FURS

New Fall Dresses

At Popular Prices

$19.50, $25, $29.50, $35, $40

New Fall Coats

$15, $17.50, $19.50, $23.50, $25

New Fall Suits

$30, $32.50, $35, $37.50, $40

FINAL CLEARANCE

Every Suit, Coat, Dress

1/4—1/3—1/2 of the Original Price

SUITS

COATS

DRESSES

Now $6.75 to $37.50

WASH DRESSES

This August 10, 1913, issue of *The Call* announced that 23 women graduated from the first vocational training class at the Emporium. They studied "textiles, silks, woolens, cotton, linens, business arithmetic as applied to store work, store service and hygiene for women . . . They have been taught how to approach customers, how to display their goods to their best advantage, and how to give the best and most efficient service and eliminate mistakes in making change and in delivering packages." (Courtesy of the Library of Congress, Chronicling America.)

San Francisco Gas & Electric Company, the precursor to today's Pacific Gas & Electric Co., suffered significant infrastructure loss in the earthquake. By 1910, when this ad appeared, the utility was touting the fact that the Emporium chose to use them to supply all the electricity for its mammoth operation. (Courtesy of the Library of Congress, Chronicling America.)

Andrew Bernard Charles "A.B.C." Dohrmann (1868–1936), son of F.W. Dohrmann, was involved in the affairs of the Emporium starting with its reorganization and expansion in 1897. He was elected president in 1916 and became chairman in the 1930s. Like his father, he was involved in many other business and civic activities, including being one of the founders of Yosemite Park Company before its merger with the Curry Company around 1925. (Courtesy of Mark Dohrmann.)

This 1912 view of Powell Street looking toward Market Street and the Emporium shows a cable car going south. The St. Francis Hotel is on the right, and Union Square is on the left, just out of frame. Construction materials at the right indicate that the addition to the third wing of the St. Francis is being constructed. (Photograph by Hamilton Henry Dobbin; courtesy of the California History Room, California State Library, Sacramento, California.)

This 1919 night view shows the St. Francis Hotel illuminated with strings of lights. In the foreground, Union Square is also lit up and decorated with a row of columns. F.W. Dohrmann of the Emporium was one of the organizers of the San Francisco Hotel Company, which operated the St. Francis. (Photograph by Hamilton Henry Dobbin; courtesy of the California History Room, California State Library, Sacramento, California.)

After America entered World War I, one could not escape from the "Buy a bond" slogan. Boy and Girl Scouts primarily sold the bonds, selling 2,328,308 Liberty bonds between 1917 and 1918. In the photograph above, ladies sell the bonds at a table on Market Street, near the Emporium. In the photograph to the left, the view looks southeast across Union Square. The Dewey Monument, surrounded by a crowd including a Red Cross nurse, is decorated with patriotic bunting and wrapped in a sign urging people to buy Liberty Bonds. The City of Paris store is visible directly behind it. (Both photographs by Hamilton Henry Dobbin; courtesy of the California History Room, California State Library, Sacramento, California.)

In September 1919, Pres. Woodrow Wilson and his wife toured the country as part of his unsuccessful effort to win support for American entry into the League of Nations. Here, the president and his wife drive up Market Street, escorted by cavalry, marines, and sailors. Cheering throngs lined the streets. (Photograph by Hamilton Henry Dobbin; courtesy of the California History Room, California State Library, Sacramento, California.)

During World War I, the Red Cross sought donations for the relief effort abroad. Volunteers staffed enrollment booths, found on street corners at all hours, to solicit subscribers, while some local communities organized parades and pageants. Here, volunteers collect funds for the Red Cross on Market Street. (Photograph by Hamilton Henry Dobbin; courtesy of the California History Room, California State Library, Sacramento, California.)

Before ready-to-wear clothing became more available during and after World War I, department stores featured vast fabric departments on their ground floors. This 1915 photograph shows bolts of silk, woolens, and cotton on the main floor of the Emporium. Clerks and buyers learned about quality, grades, prices, and sources. Many fabrics were imported from Europe and the Far East; American mills made less-expensive cottons and wool blends. As this photograph shows, the sales personnel were usually male, and, if they were successful, advanced to buyer positions. These "dry goods men" had to know the difference between different silks, how many yards were needed for a certain kind of jacket, and the wearing properties of velveteen. After ready-to-wear clothing became more available, the fabrics, silks, and ribbons often moved to a higher floor, and fast-selling items such as jewelry, handbags, and perfume moved to the ground floor. (Courtesy of the California Historical Society, CHS2013.1456.)

The mid-19th-century department stores in New York, Paris, and San Francisco perfected the art of visual merchandising, primarily aimed at women. As consumer demand and disposable income grew, merchandisers at department stores such as the Emporium deliberately staged windows to draw people into the stores, appealing to their dreams of upward mobility. In the window at left, the Emporium displays Edwardian-style dresses, which were very popular in the early 1900s. The postcard below, from 1911, features an arcade at the store with corsets and fabrics. A 1908 *San Francisco Chronicle* article breathlessly claimed, "The glass arcade, the handsomest and grandest display windows in the world, with plate-glass exposure of 750 feet in length, unequaled anywhere, challenges the admiration of every beholder." (Left, courtesy of the California Historical Society, CHS2013.I456; below, author's collection.)

Weary shoppers rested and socialized in the Emporium's café, as waitresses in starched uniforms stood ready to bring tea or other food items. Tearooms served customers who were interested in more than a quick lunch at a soda fountain. The Emporium described its café in an ad as, "Most elegantly appointed. Prompt, efficient service, inviting environment and appetizing dishes at popular prices will make it a favorite San Francisco eating place." The photograph to the right shows the home furnishings department, with sofas and beds. (Above, author's collection; right, courtesy of the Westfield San Francisco Centre.)

A 1908 *San Francisco Chronicle* article about the store's reopening described the ground floor thusly: "The dry goods department is located at the front entrance, occupying the space at both sides of the central aisles, and reaches back two-thirds of the main floor. The shoe department, with its tall glass cases, which give it seclusion from prying eyes, is across the aisle from the dry goods department. Across the aisle from that department is one filled with the best and choicest garments for boys and children, and reaches to the department for men's clothing. There are three broad entrances facing Market Street and five aisles running parallel with the center aisle. The most complete grocery and delicatessen departments known are also located on the first floor." (Above, courtesy of the California Historical Society, CHS2013.I458; below, courtesy of the Society of California Pioneers and Louis Capecci.)

The Emporium's elevator operators pose on the roof in 1915. Elevator operators were needed to run manually-operated elevators, which were controlled by a large lever that would cause the elevator to stop or run. Department store operators often also acted as greeters and tour guides, announcing product departments floor by floor and occasionally mentioning special price offers. However, since a goal for department stores was to get shoppers to go beyond the ground floor, elevators were inefficient, as they could only carry about 400 people an hour. By the 1930s, stores were installing escalators, or "moving sidewalks," which helped solve that problem, as they could transport many more people (up to 25 times more, depending on their width) than elevators. (Courtesy of Pam Gibson.)

These Emporium poster stamps—also known as Cinderella stamps, defined as anything that looks like a normal postage stamp but is not—were part of a collecting craze prior to World War I. They were an advertiser's dream, a small advertisement, a little larger than most postage stamps, which collectors put in albums. Advertising was the driving force of poster stamps, whether it was advertising a white sale, infant wear, gloves, or ribbons. In addition to advertising products or events, stamps also promoted political causes or good works, encouraged tourism, and so forth. (Both, author's collection.)

Poster stamp societies and clubs eagerly sought these poster stamps and had exhibitions. Not only were they put in albums, they were also affixed to envelopes and invoices, given away with products, and collected to obtain other awards. Some companies even offered their own collection albums. Germany, with its stellar printing industry, was a massive producer of poster stamps. World War I was devastating to the hobby, and the craze all but disappeared. (Both, author's collection.)

"Dome Quality" became the Emporium's branded slogan for its goods, which it claimed were "the best that can be produced for the money." This 1908 ad, published soon after the Emporium reopened, read: "LOOK for Dome Quality! DEMAND Dome Quality! BUY Dome Quality!" The ad also announced the reopening of four departments, including the "Oriental Department, Candies, Domestic and Oriental rugs and Millinery—Authentic Styles, Rich and Exclusive." In describing its gowns, "Direct Paris Importations," the ad said, "It is impossible to describe these gowns. The most harmonious effects, rich fabrics, valuable laces, beautiful heavy soft satin, exquisite embroideries, gold laces and garnitures are only secondary matters to carry out the wonderful originality and artistic conception of the designer." (Courtesy of the Library of Congress, Chronicling America.)

THE SAN FRANCISCO CALL, THURSDAY, SEPTEMBER 14, 1911.

FALL FASHION SHOW

The Emporium

September 14·15·16

The whole town interested in the Fashion Show, and the Fashion Show at The Emporium this year means more than ever before. Preparations made on a much larger scale. Representatives were sent abroad months in advance. A large percentage of the show gowns, hats and wraps, bought in Paris and shipped through direct in bond to The Emporium, San Francisco. Other European cities ransacked by our people contribute in a hundred ways to novelties and show pieces. It is thus The Emporium gives the first knowledge of oncoming fads and new fashions, for to look is to know. Most authentic display. Correct toilettes shown in Fashion Promenade on living model.

Treasures in Gowns

Immense stocks of smart, practical up to date suits, coats, wraps, adaptations from foreign models or clever conceptions of our own designers, at popular prices, are set off by exquisite garments modeled by the world's most famous designers. A few of the many:

From Agnes

Callot Soeurs

From Paquin

From Rouff

From Poiret

Dœillet Brandt

From Doucet

Hats Are Beautiful Beyond Description

Those from abroad were chosen by our own expert, who came home bubbling with ideas which were liberally imparted to our own designers, who have so cleverly carried them out as to make Emporium creations vie with those from such designers as Caroline, Reboux, Georgette, Maria Guy, Germaine, Suzanne Talbot, Marie Croizet, Maison Royant and others. First tendencies show the small and medium size hats with extremely high crowns and trimming, later the ultra smart, huge flat hats. Whether it is an original Parisian creation you wish or a clever adaptation, we feel assured we were never better able to serve you or to offer such gorgeous materials to select from.

Blouses—A Prominent Feature in Fall Fashions

Beautifully wrought in Irish laces, intricately designed nets or Bizarre effects in the multi-colors. For the conservative woman are the soft, delicately shaded chiffons, pure whites and solid blacks, that are wonders in construction and design. Sashes are a style note bound to find favor. Drapes are largely used, and are picturesque and becoming.

Exquisite Materials for the Making

Accessories in Keeping for Fall

Here illustrated two imported robes by Paquin and Poiret

The sketch was executed by

Miss Bertha M. Boye, the winner of the $100 prize Fashion Show poster

Bertha M. Boye

This elegant ad promoted Fashion Week and French gowns shows: "Two imported robes by Paquin and Poiret." By 1911, the idealized Edwardian image of the Gibson Girl, from Charles Dana Gibson's 1890s illustrations, was on the wane. Gibson Girls wore very tight corsets to create an hourglass figure. Their straight-front corsets pushed the rear back and the bosom forward, creating the "S-bend." As the Edwardian Age drew to a close, women demanded freedom of movement by loosening their corsets and getting rid of the trains. This was healthier because it was less restrictive, and also popular because of its naturalness. *Modern Priscilla*, a popular monthly women's magazine, reported in 1911 that "This season the straight up-and-down silhouette is the fashionable one, the aim being to give the effect of an un-corseted figure." (Courtesy of the Library of Congress, Chronicling America.)

Neckwear

Closed Today Washington's Birthday

The Emporium

Sales Begin Tomorrow Morning 8:30 o'clock

E. & W. Collars

2 for 25c

New Tailored Suits and Beautiful Models of Colored Linens

At $30 and $35

At $50 and $55

At $40 and $45

At $60 to $100

$17.50 to $75.00

Specials : $5.00

One of the Most Noted of The Emporium's Silk Sales

45¢

48¢

Special at 45c the Yard

Special at 48c the Yard

The Last Week of the Curtain Sale

Sale of Jewelry at Just 1/2 Price

Oriental Rugs at 25% Discount

38c

$1.00

$2.50

$1.65

New Ribbons

Jet Jewelry Novelties

The Emporium's Great Sale of "Nine Cent Wash Goods"

One of the Greatest Sales of Yard Goods San Francisco Has Ever Seen, At This Price

9¢

Splendid Values in Light Percales

Thousands of Yards of Dark Percales

See Our Window Display Sunday and Monday

Take Advantage and Buy in Large Quantities

"Nothing to Do but the Sewing on These Pretty Frocks" read the ad in the center of the page, promoting "semi made dresses. Everything is pre-cut for the busy mother, and includes "belt, button, trimming and full directions." In 1911, the move towards more ready-to-wear was underway, and the Emporium claimed that it was the first to introduce these kits in San Francisco. (Courtesy of the Library of Congress, Chronicling America.)

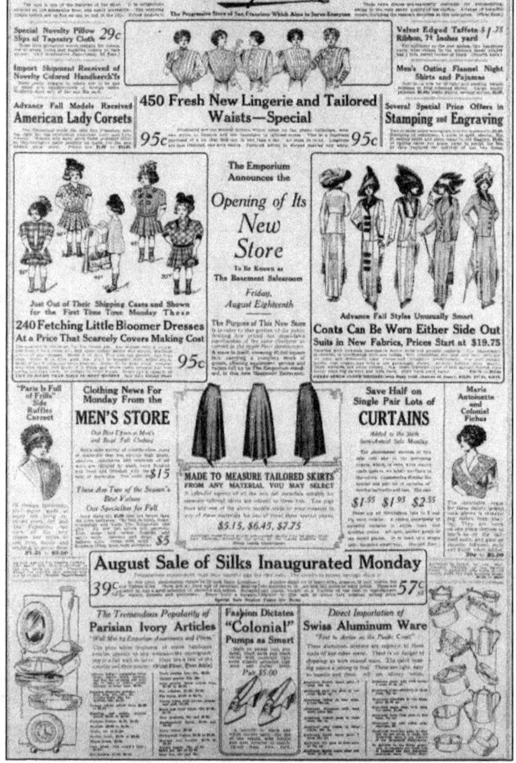

The Emporium

450 Fresh New Lingerie and Tailored Waists—Special

95c

American Lady Corsets

Stamping and Engraving

The Emporium Announces the Opening of Its New Store

To Be Known as The Basement Salesroom

Friday, August Eighteenth

240 Fetching Little Bloomer Dresses

At a Price That Scarcely Covers Making Cost

95c

Coats Can Be Worn Either Side Out

Suits in New Fabrics, Prices Start at $19.75

MEN'S STORE

CURTAINS

MADE TO MEASURE TAILORED SKIRTS

$5.15, $6.45, $7.75

August Sale of Silks Inaugurated Monday

39c

57c

Parisian Ivory Articles

"Colonial" Pumps as Smart

Swiss Aluminum Ware

Post-earthquake growth continued. This 1911 ad announced the opening of the Basement Salesroom on August 18, 1911. Its stated purpose was "to cater to that portion of the public desiring low priced but dependable merchandise of the same character as carried in the upper floor departments." (Courtesy of the Library of Congress, Chronicling America.)

Four

THE 1920s AND 1930s
SURVIVING THE ECONOMIC DOWNTURN

During the postwar 1920s, the Emporium's fast growth continued. Americans' standard of living kept rising, and what better way to spend money than on household goods, clothing, and luxury items such as wristwatches, electronics (phonographs and radios), perfumes, and cosmetics? Nearly 2,000 employees worked the Emporium's 600,000-square-foot store. Sales reached $16.8 million in 1925. It was an exciting time for America and for retail.

In 1927, plans were in the works for a Bay Bridge linking San Francisco to the East Bay (completed in 1936), and expanding to the East Bay made sense. That year, to great fanfare, the Emporium merged with the H.C. Capwell Company of Oakland, forming a holding company, the Emporium-Capwell Company.

Harris Cebert "H.C." Capwell was an Oakland institution. In 1899, he opened a small store there called The Lace House. It changed its name to the H.C. Capwell Company two years later, moved to larger quarters, and, as time progressed, was recognized as one of the leading retail stores in the Bay Area. By 1929, the merged organization had built a six-story building that became Capwell's largest store, located on a block of land in downtown Oakland.

The two divisions merged their New York and overseas buying offices, but operated their stores independently for many years.

By the late 1920s, chain stores such as J.C. Penney and Sears were on the rise. J.C. Penney had four stores in 1908 and 1,452 by 1930. Sears, Roebuck & Co., which started as a mail-order house, opened its first eight retail stores in 1925 and operated 338 by 1930. Sears established its stores away from large cities, with expansive parking lots. Downtown department stores such as the Emporium faced daunting challenges as their costs increased, traffic snarled the roadways, and customers chose to move to the suburbs. Then the 1929 stock market crash and the ensuing Great Depression hit, and consumers' disposable income all but evaporated. However, the Emporium weathered the downturn, enticing customers with visits from celebrities, radio programs, Christmas festivities, a traveling exhibition of "Treasures of the Czars," and a 1931 exhibit featuring a 54-foot replica of the Golden Gate Bridge.

In the 1920s, San Francisco was growing; it was no longer hemmed in by Bernal Heights on the south and Twin Peaks on the west, and development was spreading into the Sunset District, the Outer Mission, the Bayview District, and other areas. Electric streetcars carried hundreds of thousands of passengers on the Market Street Railway Company in 1924, transporting them to the Emporium and down to the Embarcadero. (Author's collection.)

Shoppers stroll in Union Square in the 1920s. After post-earthquake reconstruction, the square's retail area became even more vital. This image shows the Dewey Monument (named after Spanish-American War hero Adm. George Dewey) in the middle of the square, the St. Francis Hotel, and the Fitzhugh Building, which was built in 1923 and mainly contained offices. (Courtesy of the California History Room, California State Library, Sacramento, California.)

In the middle of downtown San Francisco, the Emporium had a seed and nursery shop. During World War I, there was a slogan, "Food as important as men or munitions." Garden clubs sprang up everywhere, and in free lectures, people learned how to prepare, plant, and cultivate whatever ground they could get, from small backyards to vacant lots. This interest in gardening continued into the 1920s and 1930s. (Courtesy of the San Francisco History Center, San Francisco Public Library.)

Workers place blue cypress and boxwood trees along the curb in front of the Emporium, getting ready for the Golden Gate International Exposition (1939–1940), a world's fair held at San Francisco's Treasure Island. The mayor's Citizens City Beautiful Committee urged the "reforestation" of Market Street so the city would look its best for the big fair. (Courtesy of the San Francisco History Center, San Francisco Public Library.)

These elegant ladies in their fur coats stand in the entryway to the Emporium. Furs in the 1920s often included large fur collars, wrapping collars, or wrapped coats (what the French call *manteau enveloppe*). During the decade, advances in mink and fox ranching helped perfect the science of mutation colors, which had already started in the late 19th century. (Courtesy of Jim Dickson.)

Read inside for one of the most important Fashion announcements of the year!

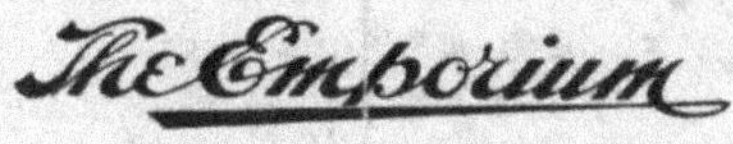

Market Opposite Powell
San Francisco

The Roaring Twenties were a time of great prosperity and ushered in an era of luxury as the economy boomed after World War I. Advertising at the time reflected the wealth of the nation, and department stores sought to distance themselves from their bargain basement reputations and remake themselves as style leaders. Consumers had grown wary of stores that had sale after sale. Department stores, watching the growth of competition like the chain stores outside the city centers, increased their advertising budgets, enhanced their radio programming, and did targeted special mailings like this Emporium fur direct mail piece. (Both courtesy of Jim Dickson.)

You are invited to a

One day private sale, Saturday, July 5

in The Emporium's Auditorium

$100,000 worth of Fall Fur Coats at prices not equalled in fourteen years- our greatest single event

which will not open to the public until Monday, July 7

$100 $150 $195

Represented in the entire collection are:

Choice natural Siberian squirrel, [illegible]-dyed squirrel, Hudson seal (dyed muskrat) caracul, leopard cat, African kid caracul, American broad-tail, caracul paw, pony, silver muskrat, back muskrat, pony paw, lapin, sealine (dyed coney).

New flattering collars and cuffs, in summer ermine, beaver, squirrel, fox, badger, wolf. Flared flounces, coats with slightly fitted lines. Each coat requires one-fourth more fur than before. All are beautifully lined in heavy satin or silk crepe.

Coats purchased will be stored in our scientifically treated vaults 'til November 1st if you wish.

Budget terms may be arranged. Ten per cent down, ten equal payments, plus a small carrying charge.

Mannequins will model fur coats all day Saturday.

Don't Forget! This event will be held in The Emporium Auditorium

VIPs gather to celebrate the merger with H.C. Capwell in 1927. The sign announces the future building of the Capwell headquarters, an entire city block at Twentieth and Broadway Streets in Oakland. A.B.C. Dohrmann, president of the Emporium, declared, "This magnificent new building with its 12 acres of floor area will soon be the home of the greater H.C. Capwell department store and will stand as an enduring monument to the splendid achievement of your foremost citizen and my good friend, Mr. H.C. Capwell." The store opened there in August 1929. Fourth from the left is A.B.C. Dohrmann. Fourth from the right is Albert John Evers, an architect with Ashley & Evers who was involved in designing various Dohrmann commercial buildings, including the Trinkler-Dohrmann Building in downtown San Jose, which is now listed in the National Register of Historic Places. (Above, courtesy of the Bancroft Library, University of California, Berkeley, 91/29c ctn 1:34; below, author's collection.)

SFU1334

THE EMPORIUM CAPWELL COMPANY

INCORPORATED UNDER THE LAWS OF THE STATE OF CALIFORNIA

This Certifies that **LOUIS HECHT EHRLICH** is the owner of **ONE HUNDRED EIGHTY ONE**

FULLY PAID AND NON-ASSESSABLE SHARES OF THE PAR VALUE OF $10.00 EACH OF THE COMMON STOCK OF THE EMPORIUM CAPWELL COMPANY, transferable in person or by duly authorized attorney upon surrender of this Certificate properly endorsed. On the reverse of this Certificate and made a part hereof, is a statement of the rights, preferences, privileges and restrictions granted to or imposed upon the respective classes and series of shares and upon the holders thereof. This Certificate is not valid until countersigned by the Transfer Agent and registered by the Registrar.

Witness the seal of the Corporation and the signatures of its duly authorized officers.

Dated JAN 31 1963

SECRETARY

PRESIDENT

CROCKER-ANGLO NATIONAL BANK

In 1931, a Progress Exposition detailing San Francisco's $258 million construction program opened at the Emporium. A 54-foot miniature Golden Gate Bridge was on display, spanning the main aisle under the Emporium dome. Other projects in the exhibition included the Hetch Hetchy dam, the San Francisco War Memorial, and many government buildings. (Courtesy of the San Francisco History Center, San Francisco Public Library.)

In 1934, a 65-foot model of the San Francisco–Oakland Bay Bridge was displayed in the window of the Emporium. A *San Francisco Chronicle* reporter wrote, "Besides the model, the exhibit includes a mastodon tooth, found 180 feet below the floor of the bay, a sample of cable from which the bridge will hang, a diver's outfit, and samples of construction materials." (Courtesy of the San Francisco History Center, San Francisco Public Library.)

This 1934 street view of the Emporium was taken when the country was in the midst of the Great Depression. Total retail sales in the country dropped from $48.5 to $24.5 billion from 1929 to 1933. In 1932, unemployment had reached 23.6 percent, and peaked in early 1933 at 25 percent. Department stores implemented stringent cutbacks and did whatever they could to keep sales up. Price came first, and style second. (Courtesy of the San Francisco History Center, San Francisco Public Library.)

Emporium employees in the 1920s gather on the rooftop in costumes. In the 1920s, stores paid more attention to their public image, increased wages, and provided club rooms and other amenities for workers. In 1925, the Emporium purchased an 82-acre country club in Marin County, where employees could swim and play golf, tennis, and baseball. To inaugurate a sale or a special event, the store would hold employee dances before the store opened. (Courtesy of Craig Sundstrom.)

The Depression hit California hard. The unemployment rate, only 3 percent in 1925, was 25 percent in 1933. To get out and find some fun amidst the gloom, people would come to the Emporium; "Meet me under the Dome!" they would say. The Emporium dome lent an air of glamour, and it was an ideal place to meet friends, hear a concert, or have tea in downtown San Francisco. This 1935 photograph shows a full orchestra playing in the rotunda, with a Hawaii promotion (note the tall palm trees) in the display area behind them. Perhaps this display was promoting Pan American China Clipper starting transpacific service in 1935, from Alameda to Manila with overnight stops at Honolulu, Midway, Wake, and Guam. Onlookers crowd the aisles and the balconies. (Courtesy of the San Francisco History Center, San Francisco Public Library.)

July 1934 was a violent month of labor unrest in San Francisco. A general maritime strike had paralyzed all shipping up and down the Pacific Coast for more than two months. On Bloody Thursday, July 5, 1934, San Francisco police killed two strikers. Four days later, tens of thousands of strikers and sympathizers marched up Market Street for a mass funeral. The general strike that followed effectively shut down both San Francisco and Oakland. The big department stores remained open but unpatronized. In the image above, a newspaper vendor announces in front of the Emporium that the strike is over. At left, police captain Albert Munn of Southern Station tells a picket captain to stop blocking the sidewalk. (Above, courtesy of the Bancroft Library, University of California, Berkeley, BANC PIC 1959.003:143—PIC; left, courtesy of the San Francisco History Center, San Francisco Public Library.)

Despite the dismal economy, the store continued to innovate. Here, crowds of people wait to ride the new escalator, or "moving staircase." In 1936, the Emporium installed escalators costing $300,000 in anticipation of the crowds who would be visiting for the 1939 Golden Gate International Exposition, which had 130,000 visitors on its first day in February 1939. The new escalators could transport 8,000 people per hour and were 382 feet in total length. The fair stimulated business significantly, with one chamber of commerce publication estimating that it brought $100 million of new money into the Bay Area. (Both courtesy of the San Francisco History Center, San Francisco Public Library.)

Department stores set out to create a welcoming environment for women, their target customers. Prior to 1860, toilets for women in business districts were extremely rare. By 1937, lounges in stores like the Emporium were designed to make women feel at home, with carpets, comfortable chairs, writing materials, newspapers, and sometimes even an area for napping. (Courtesy of the San Francisco History Center, San Francisco Public Library.)

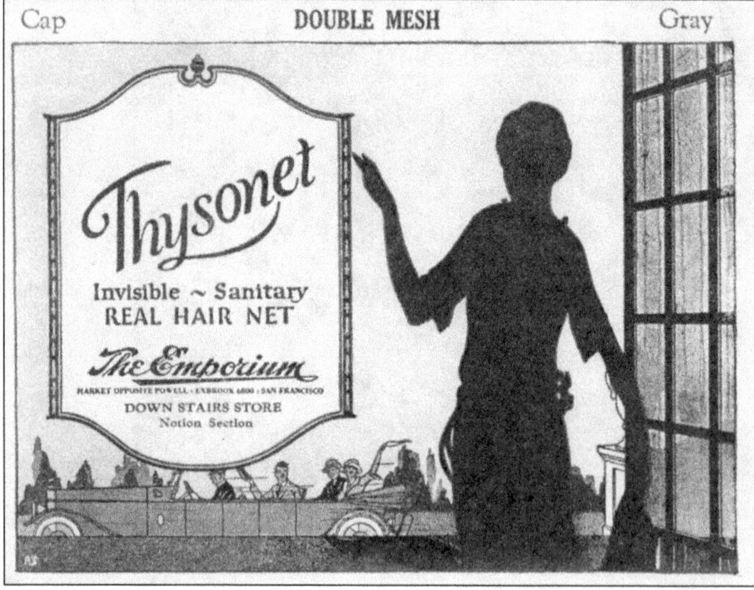

Seen here is a hair net package with Emporium branding from the 1920s. As *Inspiration* magazine said in the 1925 article "Selecting a Hairstyle," "A hair net is usually desirable, for neatness is much to be preferred to wisps of hair stringing about the face or down the back of the neck . . . it has more light and beauty if softly, and somewhat loosely, arranged." (Author's collection.)

Five

THE 1940S AND 1950S
WARTIME EFFORTS AND SUBURBAN EXPANSION

The early 1940s were all about wartime and supporting the troops. After Pearl Harbor was attacked on December 7, 1941, Emporium employees were busy blacking out the dome, windows, and light wells, organizing for civic defense, enrolling in first aid classes, and saying goodbye to more and more employees as they entered the service. From 1942 to 1945, the American Women's Voluntary Service bond booth sold bonds on the first floor. In the fall of 1945, with the war over, the Emporium was able to complete some deferred maintenance: for the first time since before the war, it was possible to clean, repair, and paint the front of the store, a sign of peaceful days again.

By 1940, there was an acute parking shortage in downtown San Francisco because of downtown development and the increasing use of automobiles. Within the area between Market and Sutter Streets, there were 17 large retail stores, 11 office buildings, 88 hotels, 15 clubs, and 7 theaters, and the capacity of nearby garages could barely serve the customers of a single store. The Union Square garage, two blocks from the Emporium, was finished by the summer of 1942, and it was only because of its alternate use as a bomb shelter and an emergency hospital that special materials were released for the building's completion.

In the years following World War II, the move to the suburbs and population growth created the need for more convenient retail shopping. Families moving to new housing developments away from city centers wanted shopping options, so the Emporium began its aggressive branch store expansion throughout the Bay Area. On April 12, 1950, it broke ground in the Stonestown Shopping Center in western San Francisco for the first branch store, six miles from its downtown parent. The three-level store, with extensive parking areas, opened in 1952. The company continued its rapid expansion into the suburbs with Capwell's Walnut Creek (1954), the Stanford Center Store (1956) in Palo Alto, Capwell's Hayward (1957), and Emporium Stevens Creek (1957). Each of the stores had over 200,000 square feet of space for goods and services and lots of room for parking.

Postwar Market Street, seen here in 1952 with the Emporium on the right, boomed. After World War II, many American military personnel who had fallen in love with San Francisco when passing through on their way to the Pacific settled in the city, prompting the creation of new neighborhoods and even more demand for consumer goods. (Courtesy of the San Francisco History Center, San Francisco Public Library.)

In 1947, after its tow broke down at First and Market Streets and held up westbound streetcar traffic for half an hour, this Navy F7F twin-engine, carrier-based plane veered to the other side of the street, hooked itself on a theater marquee, and stalled streetcars headed east. After it cleared the marquee, it swung back again across the street and promptly got hung up in a rut in front of the Emporium, as shown here. (Courtesy of the San Francisco History Center, San Francisco Public Library.)

Across the street from the Emporium, two cable car lines, Powell-Hyde and Powell-Mason, travel up from Market Street on Powell Street to Union Square and beyond. These single-ended cars must be rotated to the reverse direction at each end of the line, an operation performed on turntables with help from passengers, as seen in this 1949 photograph. (Photograph by Marshall Moxom; courtesy of the SFMTA Photograph Archive, ©2011 SFMTA, www.sfmta.com/photograph.)

In May 1950, workers prepare to lower a new deck onto the turntable for the Powell and Market Street cable car turnaround. In 1947, Mayor Roger Lapham had proposed the closure of the two Powell Street cable car lines. In response, the Citizens' Committee to Save the Cable Cars forced a referendum on an amendment to the city charter, compelling the city to continue operating the Powell Street lines. (Courtesy of the Library of Congress.)

The photograph above shows Union Square, which continued to be the city's major shopping center, featuring higher-end stores, in the 1940s. The St. Francis Hotel, on Powell Street, is at the left. People are sitting on benches and on the grass, and standing around the Dewey Monument, and palm trees line the perimeter of the park. The photograph of Union Square below shows the entrances to the underground parking garage built during the war, which not only provided badly needed parking spaces, but also could serve as a bomb shelter. Powell and Post Streets are seen, along with the St. Francis Hotel, the Four-Fifty Sutter Building, the Fitzhugh Building, the Sir Francis Drake Hotel, and the Plaza Hotel. (Both courtesy of the California History Room, California State Library, Sacramento, California.)

In September 1946, pickets paraded in front of the Emporium as part of a strike against 22 leading stores. While consumer prices had risen during the war, wages had not. When the war ended, the country was overtaken by a wave of strikes demanding higher wages. Many employees went through the lines, and the store stayed open for business. (Courtesy of the San Francisco History Center, San Francisco Public Library.)

William B. Reagan Jr., deputy administrator of the defense savings staff in Northern California, addressed employees of the Emporium at a 1942 defense bond rally in the store. A two-day bond drive in 1945 enabled the Emporium to send a check to the Treasury Department, the maturity value of which exceeded $250,000. (Courtesy of the San Francisco History Center, San Francisco Public Library.)

Wartime preparations included designing and building a special fire equipment truck at the Emporium. Two employees who had been trained to fight fire at the store in case of an air raid demonstrated the equipment in 1942. (Courtesy of the San Francisco History Center, San Francisco Public Library.)

Here, an ad announced that heavyweight boxing champion Gene Tunney would be signing copies of his 1941 book, *Arms for Living*, his second autobiography. Tunney talked about his family as well as his military and boxing careers, and offered advice to the World War II military sailors and soldiers about perseverance. (Courtesy of Jim Dickson.)

A cable car, purchased from the city, was hoisted up past the third floor of the Emporium in 1946. An employee at the window got an unusual view. The cable car was traveling up to the Emporium's roof garden, where it was to be a "memoriam to the early days of California," according to a store press release. (Courtesy of the San Francisco History Center, San Francisco Public Library.)

This 1945 advertisement promoting California-made ceramics featured a Carmen Miranda–like fruit bowl (Miranda was a popular actress and film star from the 1930s to the 1950s). By the summer of 1944, because of wartime scarcities and import restrictions, supplies of china were scarce. In the postwar period, young families returned to the market to furnish their homes, and brightly colored California pottery was the rage. (Courtesy of Kathleen Manning.)

The friendly telephone operators at the Emporium could connect callers to departments within the store, as well as take orders. Traffic congestion in the downtown area, along with gasoline rationing during World War II, led to significant growth in the number of telephone orders for department stores nationwide. (Courtesy of Jim Dickson.)

In 1957, the Emporium dome got a facelift that made it as functional as it was beautiful. Workers installed a network of intricate scaffolding in the well of the 100-foot-high dome so that they could turn it into the center of a vast ventilation system. In the photograph above, a touring party of VIPs views the Big E dome. To the right, workmen install a blower. Compare the size of the workman to the blower to get an idea of how big it was. (Both courtesy of the San Francisco History Center, San Francisco Public Library.)

In 1951, the Emporium's windows displayed manikins wearing real opera costumes of such Metropolitan Opera notables as Luisa Tetrazzini, Lucrezia Bori, Mary Garden, Ernestine Schumann-Heink, and Rosa Ponselle. RCA Victor Recording Co. shipped the costumes to the store from its warehouse. (Courtesy of the San Francisco History Center, San Francisco Public Library.)

In 1958, the downtown Emporium's better dress department, the "Rose Room," featured pale taupe walls and rosy taupe furniture. Other departments on the second floor included "Colegienne Sportswear, Social Dresses, Millinery, Daytime Dresses, and the Bridal Salon." (Courtesy of the San Francisco History Center, San Francisco Public Library.)

The ladies' lounge in Stonestown, with its upholstered couches, chairs, and writing tables, was the "plushest in town," according to the caption that accompanied this 1952 photograph. Female shoppers could meet friends there, discuss the topics of the day, read the newspaper, or just rest a bit. (Courtesy of the San Francisco History Center, San Francisco Public Library.)

From the 1930s to the 1950s, Hollywood celebrities glamorized the wearing of fur coats and stoles. Even with the onset of World War II and material rationing, women still sought out fur fashions. Although the Emporium was more of a mid-range store compared to the City of Paris (founded 1850) and I. Magnin (founded 1876), both located on Union Square, it offered higher-end items such as furs in its Fur Salon. (Courtesy of the San Francisco History Center, San Francisco Public Library.)

The store had to keep innovating to keep drawing those customers. Here, it is feeding time for the penguins on display in 1951, and kids and adults look on eagerly. Other displays of the era included the first full-length x-ray photograph, a livestock exposition, 75 live birds, and two polar bear cubs. (Courtesy of the San Francisco History Center, San Francisco Public Library.)

Pedestrians crowd the front of the Emporium for what appears to be a visitation from outer space. But they found it was a promotional stunt for the Big E's Toyland. In this image, a pair of little people in space suits is welcomed by a "Flying Tigress" from the Flying Tiger Line, which delivered the couple's spaceship. (Courtesy of the San Francisco History Center, San Francisco Public Library.)

Television and radio star Jim Backus, the beetle-browed actor who gave life to the nearsighted cartoon character of Mr. Magoo and played the ascot-wearing millionaire Thurston Howell II on *Gilligan's Island*, made an appearance at the Emporium in 1958. He arrived in a "Merry Olds" to autograph copies of his book, *Rocks on the Roof.* The Emporium purchased the 1901 Oldsmobile to sell at the downtown store to "the man who has everything." Backus's book, according to a review, provided "entertaining, exaggerated glimpses of radio in the old days, Hollywood, TV, house hunting in Beverly Hills, and actors' phobias." (Courtesy of the San Francisco History Center, San Francisco Public Library.)

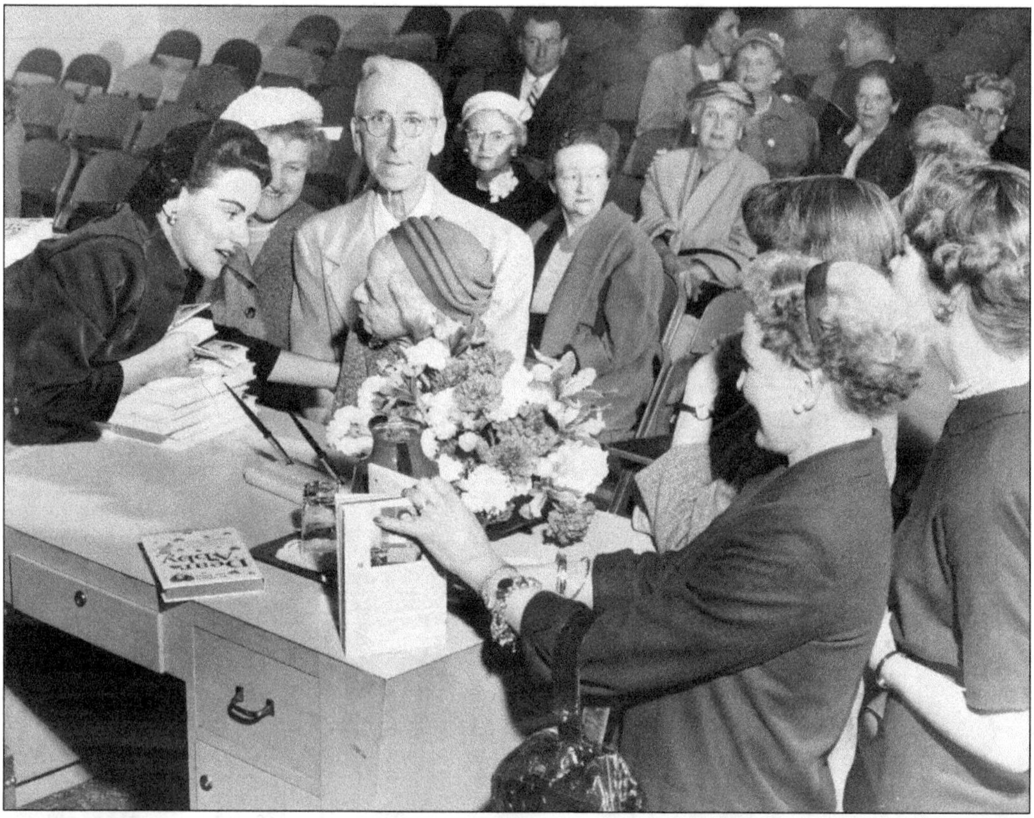

Pauline Phillips, also known as Abigail van Buren, signs copies of her book, *Dear Abby*, at the Emporium in 1958. She got her start by calling the editor of the *San Francisco Chronicle* in 1956 and saying she could write a better advice column than the one she had been reading in the newspaper. She then did some sample responses and was hired that day. (Photograph ©Bob Campbell, *San Francisco Chronicle*, Corbis.)

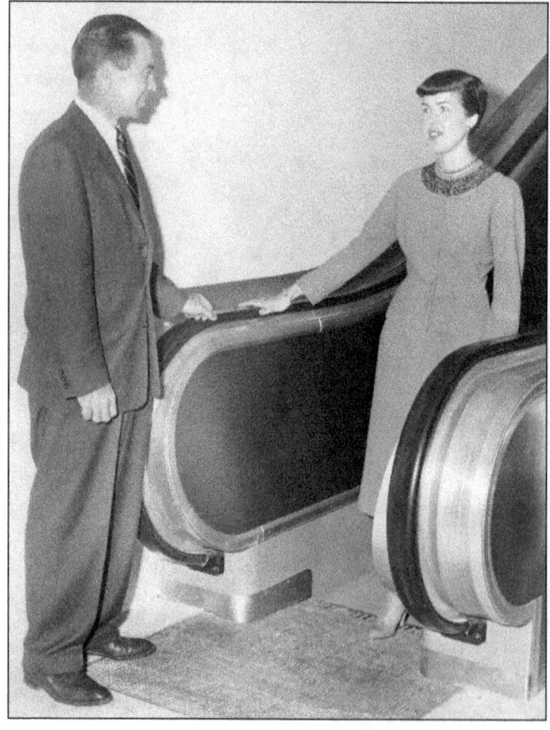

The postwar improvements continued. In 1955, the caption for this photograph announced, "Pretty Girl 'Tests' Escalator." An Emporium manager watches as a store employee takes the first ride on the store's new escalators, put in service at the rear of the downtown store. (Courtesy of the San Francisco History Center, San Francisco Public Library.)

The Emporium kept a steady stream of celebrities coming to the store. Lucius Beebe (in hat), author, gourmand, photographer, railroad historian, journalist, and syndicated columnist, and his partner, photographer Charles Clegg, signed books at an autograph party at the Emporium to introduce their book *Cable Car Carnival*. Beebe wrote articles for such periodicals as *Town & Country*, *Gourmet*, *Playboy*, *Esquire*, *Trains*, and the *San Francisco Chronicle*. Beebe and Clegg lived and traveled aboard a private railcar, *The Gold Coast*, from 1948 to 1950. The car is now part of the collection of the California State Railroad Museum. They later purchased another private car, *The Virginia City*. Clegg described Beebe as a "highly civilized 19th-century gentleman" possessing an "outrageous personal majesty," known by the world as a "wit and flamboyant gourmet." (Courtesy of the San Francisco History Center, San Francisco Public Library.)

In 1950, construction was underway for the new Emporium branch store at Stonestown, in the Lake Merced area. According to a store press release, Stonestown was the "first complete department store to be built in the San Francisco area since the war and one of the first to be traffic-engineered for customer convenience and merchandising efficiency." It represented a "pioneering experiment in store planning and design." Shown looking at a model of the new Big E (in foreground) and

other portions of the Stonestown Shopping Center are, from left to right, Welton Becket, the architect who designed the entire center; Robert Mason, manager of the store; Ellis Stoneson, project builder; E.C. Lipman, president of the Emporium-Capwell Co.; and Henry Stoneson, co-builder. (Courtesy of the San Francisco History Center, San Francisco Public Library.)

These two photographs were taken by Arnold Del Carlo, who was initially hired by the Emporium to photograph the store's merchandise so that artists could create pen-and-ink drawings for advertisements from the photographs. The Emporium also hired him in the 1950s for a series of commercial photographs, which became classics. Above, a manager makes an announcement over the public address system. Below, executives walk the aisle of the Emporium, looking at manikins wearing the latest 1950s fashions. (Both photographs by Arnold Del Carlo; courtesy of Sourisseau Academy for State and Local History, San Jose State University.)

In the late 1940s, the store underwent significant renovations, including the executive and general offices. They completely remodeled, modernized, and soundproofed the telephone exchange. In this Arnold Del Carlo photograph, store employees demonstrate the latest improvements. (Photograph by Arnold Del Carlo; courtesy of Sourisseau Academy for State and Local History, San Jose State University.)

The Emporium High School Board, seen here in 1952–1953, represented public and parochial schools in the Bay Area. Chosen by their schools and the Emporium for leadership, scholastic standing, aptitude with people, and general interest in fashion and merchandising, these 28 girls met every Saturday to learn about selling, modeling, or working on public service events at the store. (Courtesy of the San Francisco History Center, San Francisco Public Library.)

The Emporium Stevens Creek branch, at 231,000 square feet, opened in 1957 to serve the greater San Jose–Santa Clara area. This was the fifth store in the Emporium's move to establish a presence in the fast-growing suburbs. In the 1950s, two shopping centers sat side by side, with the western portion located in Santa Clara and the eastern portion of the mall located in San Jose. On the western side was an outdoor shopping center, Stevens Creek Plaza, anchored by the Emporium and I. Magnin. Valley Fair Shopping Center was confined to the eastern side of the property. Developed and anchored by Macy's, it included roughly 40 other stores, including Joseph Magnin, in an outdoor plaza. Westfield Valley Fair replaced these two separate shopping centers in the late 1990s. (Both photographs by Arnold Del Carlo; courtesy of Sourisseau Academy for State and Local History, San Jose State University.)

Open tracts outside the cramped downtown area offered endless free parking and the space to build huge stores. As part of the Emporium's ambitious expansion plans, the Emporium branch in Stonestown was the first branch of a major San Francisco department store to open outside of downtown. Officially opened in July 1952, it covered five acres and contained over 250,000 square feet of floor space. The architect, Welton Becket, and his staff spent months intensively researching the most efficient flow patterns for merchandise, store personnel, and customer traffic. They aimed to reduce to an absolute minimum the time and effort required to complete the merchandising cycle, from the delivery of goods at the unloading dock to the moment a shopper left the store with a purchase. This store location was converted to a Macy's in 1996 when Macy's bought the Emporium. (Photograph by Alan J. Canterbury; courtesy of the San Francisco History Center, San Francisco Public Library.)

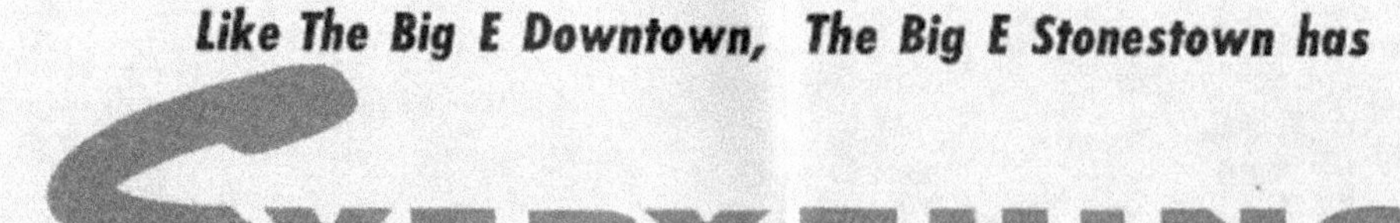

The Stonestown store had all the usual departments devoted to housewares, appliances, furniture, and clothing for men, women, and children. On the lower level was a buffet with tables for more than 200 people. In addition, there was a travel bureau and tailor shop on the mall level. The upper level had a beauty salon, classrooms for sewing and needlecraft courses, a photography studio, and a "fabulous fin de siècle" ladies' lounge, decorated like a Victorian parlor, according to a store press release. Also on the upper level were a 300-seat auditorium for special store and community events, an employees' club room, and a large roof terrace for the famed Emporium Christmas carnival. (All courtesy of Heather David.)

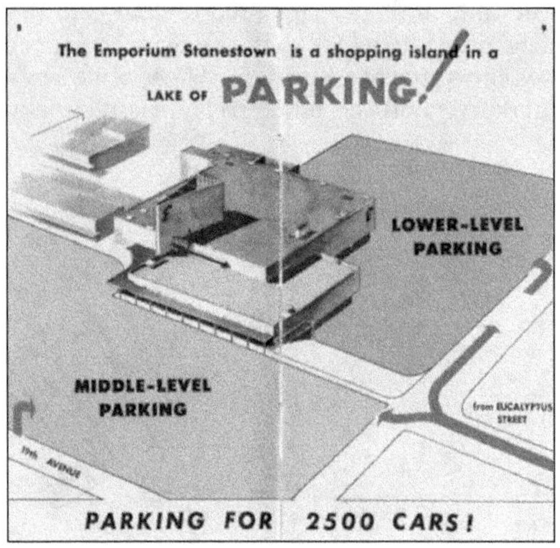

In the early 1950s, traditional media such as radio, newspapers, and magazines remained vital advertising mediums, although television was quickly becoming a cornerstone of many advertisers' media plans. The Emporium continued to produce its many catalogs, benefiting from the growing sophistication in segmenting the market. In the 1950s, direct mail was a mix of art and science, although the technological advances of the US post office helped with sorting and delivery. During the Great Depression and World War II, the post office had postponed widespread development of mechanization. In the mid-1950s, it took major steps toward mechanization, introducing its first semiautomatic parcel sorting machine. Other progress on the technology front included letter sorters, automatic address readers, advanced tray conveyors, flat sorters, and letter mail coding and stamp-tagging technology. (Courtesy of Ron Ross.)

In the early 1940s, the prewar fashions were mostly silk, satin, or cotton. During World War II, materials used to make undergarments were in short supply, so manufacturers turned to synthetic materials, which eventually led to Lycra, rayon, and Lastex (a yarn that has an elastic core wound around with cotton, silk, nylon, or rayon threads). During the 1950s, femininity with a touch of modesty was the fashion, although lingerie was a bit more risqué. Hollywood influenced fashion, as stars such as Lana Turner became known as the "Sweater Girl" because of her famous cone-shaped brassieres. Lingerie styles included bullet bras, silk slips, and high-waisted panties. Women did not wear a skirt or dress without the proper bra, panties, and slip. (Both courtesy of Ron Ross.)

Six

The 1960s and Beyond
Struggling to Survive

By 1950, virtually all major department store companies had committed to branch development, and the Emporium was no different, opening branch stores throughout the Bay Area into the late 1960s. The inner city continued to decline in the 1950s and 1960s, while the suburbs boomed. By 1969, when Broadway-Hale Stores (later Carter Hawley Hale Stores, or CHH), based in Southern California, acquired Emporium-Capwell Co., there were 11 branch stores plus the downtown Emporium in San Francisco and the H.C. Capwell Co. in Oakland. The Emporium Capwell acquisition was part of CHH's buying binge, which included Neiman Marcus and the Walden Book Co. CHH tripled sales between 1968 and 1973 and, in 1984, was the sixth-largest department store chain firm in the United States.

Disaster struck in 1989 when the San Francisco earthquake damaged most of the Emporium stores. All closed temporarily, and the downtown Oakland store remained closed for most of its fiscal year. By 1991, burdened by significant debt from its too-rapid expansion and unable to refurbish the stores to keep up with the competition and retailing trends, CHH sought bankruptcy protection.

Despite a reorganization under financier Sam Zell, renaming the corporation Broadway Stores, the company still struggled. In August 1995, Federated Department Stores, which owned Macy's, acquired Broadway Stores. Federated dissolved the chain in 1996 and consolidated the former Emporium, Broadway, and Weinstock's stores, along with its own Macy's California and Bullock's chains, to form Macy's West. The grand dame of Market Street was no more.

The beautiful building sat sadly empty until September 2006, when the Westfield San Francisco Centre, a $440 million retail-office-entertainment complex, opened after years of negotiations, bureaucratic wrangling, and reconstruction. The Centre, housing a Nordstrom, a Bloomingdale's, and many small stores, is 1.5 million square feet, triple the Emporium's original size, because Westfield took over adjoining space.

The developers kept the facade and restored many of the period features. Best of all, they restored the famous Emporium dome, which is now the centerpiece of a large atrium and colonnade. The Food Emporium in the lower level features the old Emporium logo.

In this 1964 photograph, workmen install a new Big E sign at the Market Street store. The pendant-shaped sign replaced the Big E flag that flew for many years on top of the Emporium. The new sign was 18 feet by 16 feet, with a gold-leaf metal frame and a double-Plexiglas face. Interior illumination made it easily visible from far down Market Street. In 1964, work had begun on the Bay Area Rapid Transit (BART) subway system, which tied up downtown Market Street for a decade. Also, the mid-Market district, west of the Emporium, lost much of its appeal when, under the 1967 Market Street Beautification Act, all of the brightly lit marquees and many neon signs were removed. BART construction meant that traffic was diverted away from the mid-Market area, and the district sank into a decline from which it is just now recovering with the technology boom. (Photograph by Skelton Photography; courtesy of the San Francisco History Center, San Francisco Public Library.)

The 1965 World Series, featuring the National League champion Los Angeles Dodgers against the American League champion Minnesota Twins, drew a crowd to watch it on a color TV at the Emporium. It was not until the mid-1960s that color sets started selling in large numbers. The Dodgers won. (Courtesy of the *St. Paul Pioneer Press*, Rogers Photograph Archive.)

This postcard shows an aerial view of two shopping centers in the early 1960s. In the upper center is Valley Fair Shopping Center, anchored by Macy's. To the left of Valley Fair is the Emporium store, which opened in 1957, later adding small stores and becoming Stevens Creek Center. (Courtesy of the California Room, San Jose Public Library.)

In the 1960s, the Emporium continued to expand, opening branches in Hillsdale, Santa Rosa, Fremont, Almaden, and other suburban locations. From 1961 to the end of 1970, over 240 regional malls were built, more than three times the number that had been constructed in the previous 15 years. Almost every mall that was opened had two anchor stores. Meanwhile, nationwide, downtown traffic problems contributed to a decline in downtown retail business. Department stores located in downtown areas, fighting the decline of the inner cities, often had to cut back on some of their amenities, such as tearooms, doormen, and children's playrooms. (Above, photograph by Hilt Hansen, Natural Color by Mike Roberts, Berkeley, Calif., courtesy of Heather David; below, photograph by Gerald L. French, published by Smith News Co., San Francisco, Calif., courtesy of Heather David.)

The Emporium in Santa Rosa was "the largest store between San Francisco and Portland," according to this catalog. It opened in 1966 with 208,000 square feet of selling space. Two floors "conveniently arranged and air-conditioned for your year-round comfort" awaited shoppers in the area of California known as the "Redwood Empire." The photograph below shows a float that the Santa Rosa Emporium employees had in the annual Luther Burbank Rose Parade & Festival, a community event that has been held since the 1890s. (Right, courtesy of Dorothy Rice; below, courtesy of Pam Gibson.)

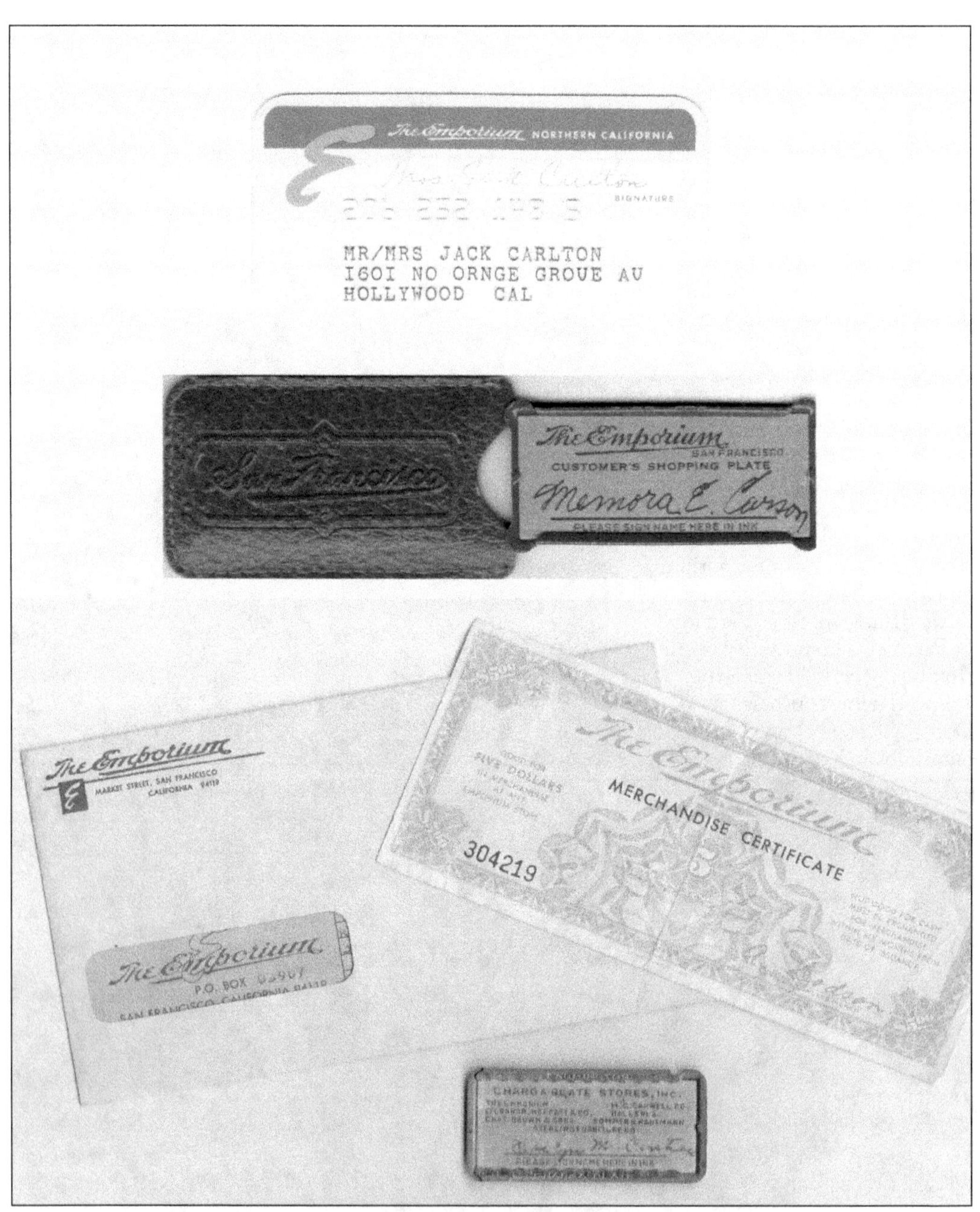

Prior to the 1950s, the larger department stores opened store charge accounts for their customers. In the early years, it was not easy to open a store credit account, and managers awarded credit only to those of solid financial standing. Of course, these accounts could only be used within the store that issued them. Early cards did not have a magnetic strip, but instead required mechanical embossers to imprint the raised information on the card onto a duplicate sales slip. It was not until Diners Club came along with a card that could be used in a large number of stores and restaurants that the credit card industry really took off. Eventually, larger stores began accepting these cards, figuring that the fees charged by the card operator were less than what it cost the store to manage their own store accounts. (Courtesy of Scott Nimmo and Ron Ross.)

Competition in the 1960s and 1970s got tougher and tougher, as the regional mall took the place of the old model of department stores, where almost everything consumers wanted could be found under one roof. Department stores became less of a distinct retail destination. The department stores responded by narrowing their offerings, focusing more on apparel, accessories, and limited household goods. The Emporium also responded by staying focused on its branding, as evidenced by this bag and the wrappers. (Right, courtesy of Jim Dickson; below, courtesy of Heather David.)

HATS CANNOT
BE RETURNED,
EXCHANGED
OR CREDITED

10-90 8-55 SF

In 1971, the Emporium published an "Album" for its employees, celebrating the "Seventy-Fifth Anniversary of the Big E Life." The cover design has elements of the rock posters of the era. The article on the back is entitled, "Dear Computer," and describes the IBM 360 Model 30 the Emporium was using for accounting and payroll. (Courtesy of Pam Gibson.)

SAN FRANCISCO BICENTENNIAL CAKE

The world's largest, tastiest and most beautiful birthday cake, 35,000 lbs., cost $100,000. Displayed in Rotunda of The Emporium Downtown.

Thirty feet high, it is decorated with 2,000 lbs. of Royal Icing depicting scenes from San Francisco's 200-year history. Topped by a five foot phoenix, the City's symbol, surrounded by 200 electric candles. The rich fruit cake, pre-wrapped in cello, is extracted by removing the handsomely decorated panels, thus leaving decor virtually intact. Recipe in part: 2,625 lbs. flour, 665 dozen eggs, 2,310 lbs. sugar, 10,745 lbs. pineapple, 8,925 lbs. cherries, 4,620 lbs. pecans, and a 220 lb. "pinch of salt".

In 1976, the Emporium featured the "world's first 35,000 pound birthday cake," intended to celebrate San Francisco's 200th birthday. Displayed in the rotunda of the Market Street store, it was topped by a five-foot phoenix—San Francisco's symbol—and surrounded by 200 electric candles. The icing had scenes of San Francisco: Miwok Indians, Spanish explorers, Franciscan friars, Mission Dolores, miners, clipper ships, Coit Tower, and more. (Cake by Centennial Cake Co.; Author's collection.)

When the Emporium on Market Street was razed in 2003, the only two architectural elements preserved were the neoclassical facade and the dome. In the photograph at right, the dome is perched on a supporting tower, waiting to be raised to the top of the new building. A custom hydraulic system lifted the 500,000-pound dome to its perch. It sat on the supporting tower for almost a year while the new structure was built underneath it. The Westfield Centre developers raised the dome to the top of the new building and removed the blockage over the windows. As part of the construction process, the dome was elevated 58 feet from its original position to allow natural light through its crown and lunette windows. There are over 800 glass panels in the dome, and more than 900 lights encased in its structural ribs. (Right, courtesy of Eric Hunt, 2004, original photograph in color; below, courtesy of the Westfield San Francisco Centre.)

Forest City Enterprises and the Westfield Group began to transform the monumental location in 2003, and it reopened in 2006. During the revitalization, they rebuilt the interior to meet stringent seismic standards. The three-story dome is again the centerpiece of a 200-foot-long, 65-foot-wide atrium and colonnade. It is 98 feet from the floor of the grand rotunda, which begins on the fourth floor, to the top of the dome's ceiling. The dome sits about 168 feet above Market and Mission Streets. The cast-iron window system, sandstone walls, columns, historic wooden windows, and glazing were completely restored. The revived street level features display windows, bronze doors, and copper piping, all elements that were part of the 1908 look of the store. Balustrades that had been removed are again prominent at the building's cornice and over the main entry of the fourth floor. (Courtesy of the Westfield San Francisco Centre.)

Seven

Christmas Rooftop Carnival

Santa's the Star

Oh, the memories. Many who grew up in San Francisco remember the rides on the roof and the Emporium holiday celebrations. The store always went to great lengths to celebrate the holidays. In the 1920s, employees distributed dolls in garlands to various charities. In 1929, the Emporium installed an organ on the south side of the dome, and music and carols rang through the store. By the 1940s, William H. Meyer, who began with Ringling-Barnum Circus in 1919, came up with the department store rooftop carnival concept, and opened his first rooftop attraction at the downtown San Francisco Emporium in 1947, followed by a similar event in Stonestown a few years later.

Santa's arrival at the beginning of the holiday season was always a big show. As a 2012 *San Francisco Chronicle* article described it, "Santa was a complete rock star . . . in terms of crowd size and fervor, it looked like a cross between a World Series victory parade and a visit by the pope. Santa always rode in style, whether it was a horse and carriage in the very early years or the Cable Car 'Santa-Cade' in the 1940s and 1950s." Parts of Market and Powell Streets were shut down and then packed with tens of thousands of people wanting to see Santa arrive. Every year, there was something special to wow the crowds, from 5,000 helium balloons to a baby elephant, a miniature horse, ice-skating queens, and assorted drummers and buglers.

On the roof, of course, kids could visit with Santa and his elves (often there were two Santas, separated by a screen). Former supervisor Angela Alioto told the *San Francisco Chronicle* in 1996, "When I was a child I thought Santa Claus lived on the roof of the Emporium." The carnival rides included a Ferris wheel, a merry-go-round, and a train. At one time, the store even had an indoor ice rink. In 1968, the carnival's giant two-humped slide was a big hit, and in the 1970s, it offered one of the city's first bouncy houses, the "Astro-Bounce." The last Christmas carnival was held in 1995, the year the store closed.

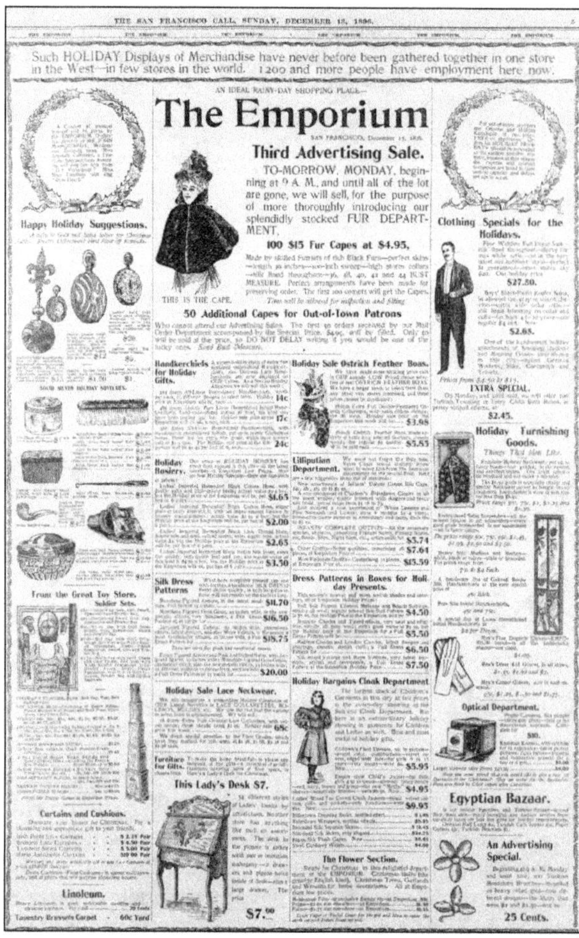

THE SAN FRANCISCO CALL, SUNDAY, DECEMBER 13, 1896.

Such HOLIDAY Displays of Merchandise have never before been gathered together in one store in the West—in few stores in the world. 1200 and more people have employment here now.

AN IDEAL RAINY-DAY SHOPPING PLACE—

The Emporium

SAN FRANCISCO, December 13, 1896.

Third Advertising Sale.

TO-MORROW, MONDAY, beginning at 9 A. M., and until all of the lot are gone, we will sell, for the purpose of more thoroughly introducing our splendidly stocked FUR DEPARTMENT,

100 $15 Fur Capes at $4.95.

THIS IS THE CAPE.

50 Additional Capes for Out-of-Town Patrons

Happy Holiday Suggestions.

Clothing Specials for the Holidays.

$27.50.

$2.65.

EXTRA SPECIAL.

$2.45.

Handkerchiefs for Holiday Gifts.

Holiday Sale Ostrich Feather Boas.

Holiday Furnishing Goods.

Holiday Hosiery.

Lilliputian Department.

From the Great Toy Store.

Silk Dress Patterns

Dress Patterns in Boxes for Holiday Presents.

Holiday Sale Lace Neckwear.

Holiday Bargains Cloak Department

Optical Department.

Furniture for Gifts.

This Lady's Desk $7.

Egyptian Bazaar.

Curtains and Cushions.

The Flower Section.

An Advertising Special.

Linoleum.

Tapestry Brussels Carpet - 60c Yard

$7.00

25 Cents.

Although Santa Claus was on hand in many department stores by the 1890s, the Emporium 1896 advertisement at left lists many holiday items but has no mention of Santa. By the early part of the next decade, Santa was showing up steadily, encouraging children to let him know what they wanted to find under the tree on Christmas morning. In the 1907 advertisement below, Santa writes to children saying he has lots of presents ready for them. They just have to write to him—care of the Emporium, of course—and let them know their wishes (and their parents' name and address). He would take care of the rest. (Both courtesy of the Library of Congress, Chronicling America.)

The Emporium

We Accept Clearing House Certificates in Payment for Merchandise or Accounts

Santa Claus' Letter Box

My Dear Children:

Christmas is coming and your old friend is getting busy again. My workmen have become so skillful and have worked so hard all the year that we have a larger and more beautiful store of presents for you than ever before. You may judge for yourselves if this is true, for they are all on exhibition at the Emporium. You know that I have been thinking for so many Christmas Eves just what I should take to you that I have not a think left in my poor old head, and I want you to help me think for you the things you most want this year.

You can do this if you will **write a little letter to me giving your name, your father or mother's name and your address,** and telling me the things you have seen at the Emporium that you would like best of all.

If you have been very good I think when you open your eyes on Christmas morning you will find Santa Claus has been thinking for you.

Address: SANTA CLAUS, at The Emporium, San Francisco, Cal.

Women's Model Suits $50.00

THE most radical and sweeping reduction that has ever been made on highest grade suits at this time of the year—in the height of the season—a reduction on beautiful new garments—most of them not in the house longer than a few weeks. Room needed to display Holiday Goods.

Suits that were marked $75 to $150, beginning Monday, all at $50

Alterations on the above garments will be extra

Closing Out the Clothing

AS announced last Friday, our entire stock of Men's, Boys' and Children's Clothing and Hats (except Stetsons) is to be closed out at once, and these departments will not be reopened until we move into our new Market Street Store late next year.

Any Suit, Overcoat or Hat (Except Stetson's) Now One-Quarter Off Marked Price

Emporium employees placed this ad in 1912 to thank management for closing the store at 6:00 p.m. during the holiday season, which they described as "a liberal stand in our behalf . . . Moreover, we know what a fortune in dollars and cents the night business means . . . we hope that our fellow workers in other stores may, in the future, enjoy the Christmas season as we have." (Courtesy of the Library of Congress, Chronicling America.)

Merry Christmas to The Emporium

The Management The Directors The Stockholders

THE EMPLOYEES OF THE EMPORIUM

We regret that the limits of the page will not admit 920 more names of loyal employes who participate in these wishes.

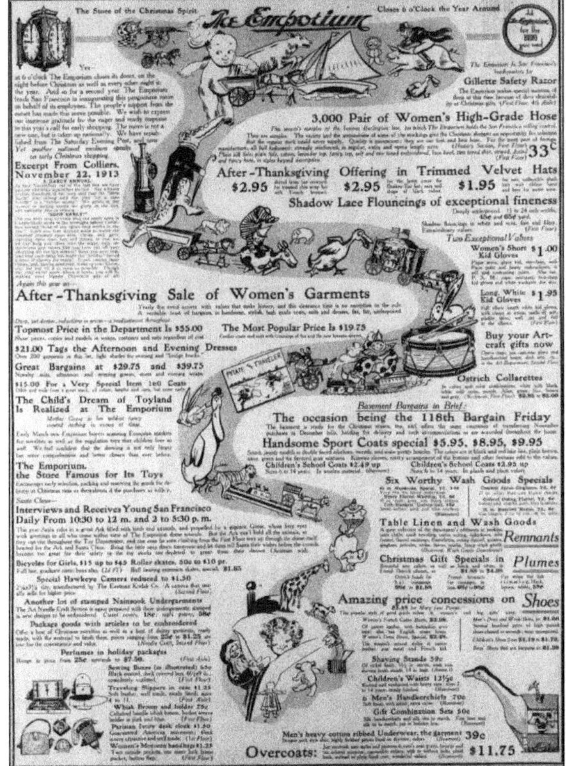

The Store of the Christmas Spirit

The Emporium

Closes 6 o'Clock the Year Around

Yes—

Excerpt From Colliers, November 22, 1913

Gillette Safety Razor

3,000 Pair of Women's High-Grade Hose 33c

After-Thanksgiving Offering in Trimmed Velvet Hats $2.95 $2.95 $1.95

Shadow Lace Flouncings of exceptional fineness

Two Exceptional Values

Women's Short Kid Gloves $1.00

Long White Kid Gloves $1.95

Again this year an—

After-Thanksgiving Sale of Women's Garments

Topmost Price in the Department Is $55.00

The Most Popular Price Is $19.75

$21.00 Tags the Afternoon and Evening Dresses

Great Bargains at $29.75 and $39.75

$15.00 For a Very Special Item 160 Coats

Buy your Art-craft gifts now

Ostrich Collarettes

The Child's Dream of Toyland Is Realized at The Emporium

The Emporium, the Store Famous for Its Toys

Santa Claus—

Interviews and Receives Young San Francisco Daily From 10:30 to 12 m. and 2 to 5:30 p. m.

Basement Bargains in Brief:

The occasion being the 118th Bargain Friday

Handsome Sport Coats special $5.95, $8.95, $9.95

Children's School Coats $2.49 up

Children's School Coats $2.95 up

Six Worthy Wash Goods Specials

Table Linen and Wash Goods Remnants

Christmas Gift Specials in Plumes

Bicycles for Girls, $15 up to $45 Roller skates, 50c to $10 pr.

Special Hawkeye Camera reduced to $1.30

Another lot of stamped Nainsook Undergarments

Package goods with articles to be embroidered

Perfumes in holiday packages

Amazing price concessions on Shoes

Shaving Stands 59c

Children's Waists 12½c

Men's Handkerchiefs 70c

Gift Combination Sets 50c

Men's heavy cotton ribbed Underwear, the garment 39c

Overcoats: $11.75

In this 1915 ad, the store announced that Santa (lower left) "rides in a great Ark, filled with birds and animals, and propelled by a giant Goose, whose fiery eyes blink greetings to all who come within view of the Emporium dome rotunda." (Courtesy of the Library of Congress, Chronicling America.)

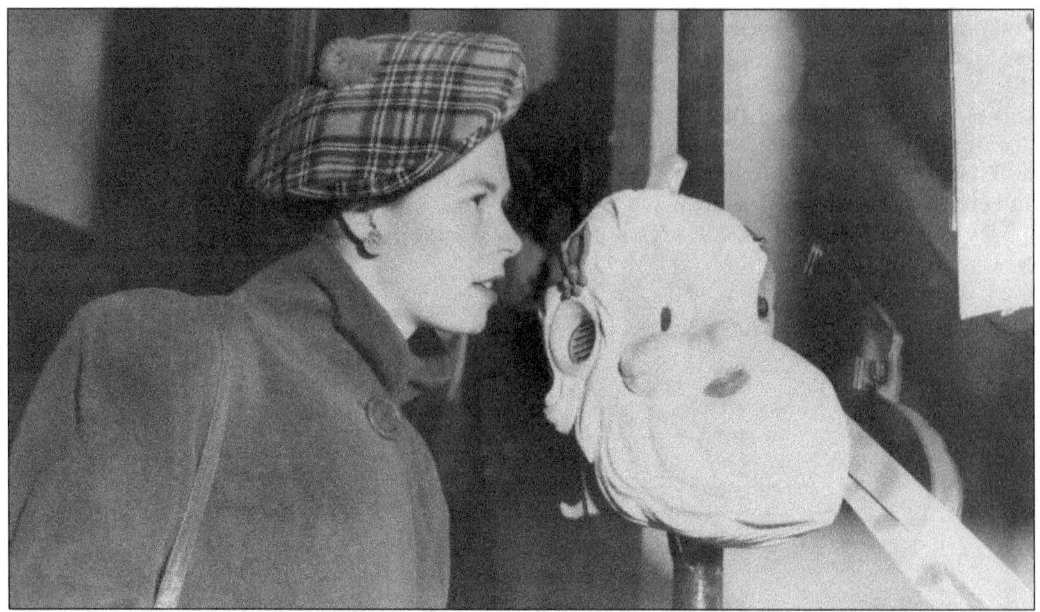

Santa was on duty 24 hours a day at the Emporium. Shoppers unable to get to the store during normal shopping hours could do their shopping by remote control. In the 1949 photograph above, a woman named Daphne Berlin gives her order to Santa, whose ear had a microphone connected to a recorder. To activate Santa, the customer would place a quarter in Santa's head, describe what she wanted and whether it was to be charged or sent Collect on Delivery (COD). The quarter was then refunded. Charging the quarter was meant to deter people who just wanted to test the voice recorder. Each morning, the mailing department would transcribe the recordings to prepare written orders and get the goods wrapped and shipped. This was actually more efficient than having children whisper to Santa what they wanted for Christmas; those interactions often did not translate into sales. (Both ©ACME News Agency, Corbis.)

The store went all-out to decorate for Christmas and prepare for Santa's arrival. The photograph above shows the front of the Market Street store in 1976. In the night shot below, two enormous Christmas trees were perched outside the fourth floor and twinkly garlands were draped all over the front of the building. Inside the store was an 80-foot tree with 12,000 lights. In 1979, it took nine engineers and 22 staff members to trim the tree with 150 ornamental baroque angels. (Above, ©Barney Peterson, *San Francisco Chronicle*, Corbis; below, courtesy of the San Francisco History Center, San Francisco Public Library.)

In November 1958, Santa, accompanied by Mrs. Claus and Jiminee Christmas, arrived atop a cable car in his "Santa-Cade," and the crowd went wild. The *San Francisco Chronicle* caption read, "Arrival of the cheerful soul—despite the heavy red overwear and high noon temperatures—at the Powell Street turntable made it official: No matter what the weather, Christmas season is here." Eight Shetland ponies, in lieu of reindeer, pulled Santa's sled. In 1955, when Santa's parade arrived, Jack Ross and his Fairmont Hotel Orchestra, dressed as Eskimos, played tunes as 5,000 balloons cascaded from the top of the store. (Above, ©Bob Campbell, *San Francisco Chronicle*, Corbis; below, photograph by Bob Warren, courtesy of the San Francisco History Center, San Francisco Public Library.)

It is November 1964, and Santa is making his big entrance once again. In August of that same year, the Beatles played south of San Francisco at the Cow Palace, which has almost 13,000 seats. Judging by this picture, it looks like Santa drew a bigger crowd. Every year, his entourage varied. One year, a dogsled accompanied him, and the Wonderland Queens in the sled waved to the crowd. Another year, 15 high school girls dressed as Christmas gnomes led the group to the store. In 1966, a baby elephant and a miniature horse, ice-skating queens, and assorted drummers and buglers kept Santa company as he made his way to the store. Santa would proclaim the opening of the Christmas season and then lead the parade to the Emporium's auditorium, which had an ice rink decorated for the season. (©Joe Rosenthal, *San Francisco Chronicle*, Corbis.)

Each fall, the University of California, Berkeley, Golden Bears football team and the Stanford University Cardinal football team square off for the "Big Game." In November 1950, fans came to a Big Game rally at a gaily decorated Emporium. Despite the wild enthusiasm of the fans of both teams, the 1950 game was a tie. (Courtesy of the San Francisco History Center, San Francisco Public Library.)

Although the downtown Emporium's Christmas festivities were a big draw, the branch stores also offered many activities. At the Stonestown store in 1956, the San Francisco Players Guild put on a performance of *Puss in Boots*. Seen here are the Enchanter and Lise, his servant. (Courtesy of the San Francisco History Center, San Francisco Public Library.)

This 1953 nighttime exposure of the lighted Ferris wheel at Christmas atop the Emporium makes it look like a giant target against the night sky. The other wheel is in the foreground, in motion but unlighted. (Photograph by Ken Adams; courtesy of the San Francisco History Center, San Francisco Public Library.)

Workmen guide a merry-go-round horse onto the roof of the Emporium in 1959, five stories above the street, as they prepare for the opening of the Emporium downtown roof rides. The carnival coincided with the opening of Toyland at all four Big E stores at the time. (Courtesy of the San Francisco History Center, San Francisco Public Library.)

Ice queens reigned on the rink in the Emporium's auditorium during the holiday season. These skaters, from the Legg Skating School troupe, presented a special "Carnival Capers" ice show in 1958. (Photograph by Romaine-Skelton Photography; courtesy of the San Francisco History Center, San Francisco Public Library.)

From the late 1920s to the late 1930s, San Francisco was a major origination point for many nationwide network broadcasts, and both NBC and CBS maintained production centers in the city. "Jolly Ben Walker," host of the popular NBC program *The Woman's Magazine of the Air*, appeared at the Emporium at Christmas to promote KGO and KPO programs and stars. (Courtesy of Ron Ross.)

Every kid in San Francisco wanted to go to the Emporium rooftop at Christmas. What a great way for the department store to cultivate the young consumer. Weary mothers on shopping trips got a break, too. In 1947 (above), there were five rides, including a train and two merry-go-rounds, as well as Santa and his helpers, of course. In 1968, Lloyd Hilligoss of Fun Fair Shows managed the rides and fair. That year, there was the Star Trek Slide (right), a Ferris wheel, a merry-go-round, a train, and a Trabant, a ride first sold in 1963 that spun horizontally and then started fluctuating like waves. (Above, courtesy of the San Francisco History Center, San Francisco Public Library; right, ©Bill Young, *San Francisco Chronicle*, Corbis.)

In 1968, the Star Trek Slide, perched on the fifth-floor roof of the Emporium, was the highest fun slide in the United States. Some of the rides were able to go up in units in the freight elevator, but not the slide, which was hoisted up outside the building. The slide, 156 feet long, 36 feet high, and 20 feet wide, had curves formed by laminated wooden archways. All the rides had to be brought up and put into action overnight. On the opening Saturday, 1,000 kids went down the slide in the first two and a half hours. (Both courtesy of *Amusement Business* magazine.)

Parents and kids line up every Christmas so the kids can tell Santa what is on their wish lists and the parents can get cute pictures for their photograph collections. Department stores and their Santa traditions go way back. It was actually a copywriter at Montgomery Ward, Robert L. May, who created a poem in 1939 about Rudolph, the ninth reindeer. Poor Rudolph, with his shiny red nose, was ostracized until he led the team of reindeers to deliver presents one foggy Christmas eve. A copy of the poem was given to Montgomery Ward customers. (Left, courtesy of Jim Dickson; top right, courtesy of Tony Ford; bottom right, courtesy of Ron Ross.)

When the early Santa Claus, or Father Christmas, first showed up in illustrations, he was not dressed in his signature red suit; sometimes it was purple, green, brown, or blue. Sometime in the late 1800s, Santa started being shown in a red suit. When Coca-Cola depicted him as a jolly fat fellow in a red suit in the 1930s, the image became the norm in American culture. (Both courtesy of Ron Ross.)

There are conflicting claims about who had the first department store Santa. Macy's claims it had an in-house Santa as early as 1862. However, the town of Brockton, Massachusetts, claims that local resident James Edgar of Edgar's Department Store was the first-ever department store Santa, in 1890. Edgar dressed up as Santa Claus based on cartoonist Thomas Nast's 1863 illustration of a jolly Santa. Edgar stated that he did it for the enjoyment of the children and to promote Christmas, not as a commercial attraction. Below, Jim Dickson, who worked at the Emporium in the 1970s, lets Santa know what is on his Christmas wish list. (Below, courtesy of Jim Dickson; right, courtesy of Ron Ross.)

www.ingramcontent.com/pod-product-compliance
Lightning Source LLC
LaVergne TN
LVHW081541100826
845153LV00004B/282

* 9 7 8 1 5 3 1 6 7 7 0 6 0 *